DIGNITY
NOT CITIZENSHIP

DIGNITY
NOT CITIZENSHIP

The Truth About Immigration
No One Is Telling You

Maria E. Salazar
MEMBER OF CONGRESS

Since 1947
REGNERY
An Imprint of Skyhorse Publishing, Inc.

Regnery Publishing books may be purchased in bulk at special discounts for sales promotion, corporate gifts, fund-raising, or educational purposes. Special editions can also be created to specifications. For details, contact the Special Sales Department, Skyhorse Publishing, 307 West 36th Street, 11th Floor, New York, NY 10018 or info@skyhorsepublishing.com

Regnery® and Skyhorse Publishing® are registered trademarks of Skyhorse Publishing, Inc.®, a Delaware corporation.

Visit our website at www.skyhorsepublishing.com.
Please follow our publisher Tony Lyons on Instagram @tonylyonsisuncertain.

10 9 8 7 6 5 4 3 2 1

Library of Congress Cataloging-in-Publication Data is available on file.

Hardcover ISBN: 978-1-5107-8656-1
eBook ISBN: 978-1-5107-8658-5

Cover design by David Ter-Avanesyan

Printed in the United States of America

Acknowledgments

This book is dedicated to two extraordinary Americans.

Jaime R. Court from Viña Del Mar, Chile. The perfect American Dream. Without his presence in my life, I would have never been able to get to Congress. My eternal gratitude for his patience, his commitment, and his emotional and financial help.

John Mark Kolb from Hoover, Alabama. A true American patriot. Without him on my congressional staff, I would have never been able to write the Dignity Act of 2025. His five years of unwavering commitment to fixing our immigration crisis—against all hope—are proof of his character and dedication. My eternal gratitude for his loyalty, his perseverance, and his faith.

Contents

President Donald Trump,

This book was written for you.

You don't have to love it.

You only have to embrace the message of dignity.

It will be the biggest legacy of your presidency.

You could be for immigration what Lincoln was for slavery and Reagan was for Communism.

May the Lord Almighty give you the divine wisdom to understand it.

Respectfully,

Congresswoman Salazar

Fifteen Things Every American Should Know About Immigration

1. Our immigration system is broken.
2. It is no longer capable of meeting the demands of our economy, it cannot keep Americans safe, and it is making life worse for all Americans.
3. Political gridlock has turned the issue into a perpetual crisis. No one wants to solve it. It's too toxic, too difficult, and too politically costly.
4. Calls for mass deportations promise toughness but guarantee disaster. Removing millions of long-term workers from the United States will devastate the economy. Without farmers and slaughterhouse workers, grocery store shelves will be empty in a week. Without builders, housing and construction will grind to a halt. Without dishwashers, cooks, and busboys, restaurants will shutter. Labor shortages will drive costs higher, fueling inflation and crushing family budgets. Mass deportations of contributing workers will not strengthen America; they will create economic chaos and negatively affect the quality of life for all Americans.

5. We need a carefully calibrated immigration solution that meets today's circumstances.
6. The way forward is the Dignity Act of 2025 (HR 4393).
7. Dignity is a revolutionary bill that unlocks unprecedented growth and stability by integrating millions of undocumented workers already contributing to our economy—requiring them to pay restitution, obey our laws, and live in the light, but without ever granting a path to citizenship. This does NOT apply to criminals, and it only applies to immigrants who arrived before 2021.
8. The Dignity Act provides no path to citizenship, no federal benefits, and no handouts. This is not amnesty.
9. Legal status and a pathway to full participation in American life will add trillions of dollars to the US economy. It will secure the future of Social Security and Medicare by expanding the tax base with millions of reliable contributors. It will close loopholes that undercut American workers and invest funds into job training and upskilling for American workers to bring a new golden age of American manufacturing and innovation.
10. Just as important: by bringing the good people out of the shadows, Dignity frees ICE and law enforcement to focus on the real threats—the drug traffickers, violent criminals, and gang networks who should be arrested and deported. It also permanently seals the border and locks in strong enforcement policies to stop illegal immigration once and for all.
11. This is not charity for the illegals. It is a permanent, onetime fix intended to strengthen the nation's borders, stop illegal immigration, reform legal immigration, and make life better for all Americans.

12. Dignity is a signal: America is still capable of solving hard problems in practical ways that restore order and uphold our values. America is still the best on the block.

13. The path forward requires courage, vision, and leadership. Half-measures and short-term fixes have kept the immigration issue alive—as a political weapon—for too long. The moment for real reform has arrived. Americans are tired of the status quo. They want solutions. Four years of chaos and caravans at the border under President Biden and the reelection of President Trump have made this extremely clear.

14. Now is the time—not just to manage immigration, but to harness it as an engine of prosperity and unity.

15. Dignity is not just the best way forward. It is the only way forward.

The Truth About Immigration

- America's immigration system is broken: economically dysfunctional, politically toxic.
- The American public is being lied to about this issue. No one is telling the real truth.
- President Trump has secured the border for now—but without Congress codifying border security into law, everything could flip with the next administration.
- Immigrants already sustain everyday American life—bringing them into the light strengthens the nation as a whole.
- Dignity is not charity—it's a onetime fix that makes immigration work for every American.

We are standing at a crossroads in this country.

Two paths. Two futures. Two Americas.

Our choice will shape this nation for generations.

Everyone is talking about immigration. Almost no one is telling the truth. The average American hears only two arguments.

On conservative outlets, Republican pundits declare, *"Kick them all out."* On CNN, mouthpieces of the left shout, *"Compassion! Let them all in."*

Two extremes. Lots of manipulations. Many lies.

Between them, the truth is suffocating.

Neither side is painting the full picture: about the American who hates illegal immigration and believes his life is worse because of it. Or about the undocumented landscaper in Pennsylvania who has lived here for seventeen years, who built a business, raised his American children, and prays in church every Sunday.

Neither side is explaining the full context about the undocumented mother of three in Miami who has spent a decade caring for someone else's children just to provide for her own, whom she has not seen in twenty years. Or about the American mother who lost her daughter to an illegal alien who should have been deported but was set free because we did not enforce our laws on the books.

Neither side speaks directly to the millions of undocumented berry pickers in Georgia, builders in North Carolina, dishwashers in New York City, and slaughterhouse workers in Iowa who keep our economy alive by doing the jobs most Americans refuse to do, even though they could.

Nor do they speak fully about the families and businesses in our towns who rely on those undocumented workers. The farmer in Washington who cannot get his harvest to market without farm hands breaking their backs on the fields for twelve hours a day. The restaurant owner in St. Louis whose doors would shut without dishwashers and cooks. The hotel in Las Vegas that wouldn't have clean rooms without housekeepers.

Neither side speaks to the American consumer—every man and woman who unknowingly depends on that hidden labor every time they sit down at a restaurant, buy fruit at the grocery store, check into a hotel, or walk into a newly built home.

Neither side is fully recognizing the frustration of millions of Americans who are upset about illegal immigration and are happy about what President Trump is doing to clean this up. Although, this topic is so polarizing, those frustrated Americans are only hearing half of the truth.

Because immigration is not just immigration. Immigration is the economy. Immigration is border security. Immigration is national security. Immigration is the American dream itself.

So who are the immigrants we're really talking about? Are they gang members from Tren de Aragua or violent criminals? Are they from the caravans that surged across the border under Biden's disastrous open-door policy? Or are they long-term, law-abiding neighbors who have built lives in our towns and cities? Who are the good *hombres*—and who are the bad ones?

That is why I wrote this book: to cut through the poison, to tell the truth, and to stop making this a binary choice between open borders and mass deportations and offer a third path.

A path that puts America and Americans first.

For decades, our broken immigration system has left undocumented families in limbo, illegal workers in the shadows, and our nation weaker. Unknown people were let into the country, and now you don't know who your neighbor is. Our cities became unsafe. Washington shrugged. Republicans failed. Democrats failed. And the American people paid the price—every family, every worker, every community left to carry the burden.

For decades, Republicans shouted about law and order, promised crackdowns, and then did nothing. Democrats preached compassion, promised reform, and then looked the other way. Administration after administration found it easier to kick the can down the road than to take a hard vote. Politicians used immigration as a campaign slogan, as a wedge issue, as a fundraising pitch—but not as a problem to solve.

While Washington bickered, American families bore the burden. The immigrant family that never knew if tomorrow would bring an ICE raid. The American family that saw their local factory close and was told it was because of "cheap labor." The community whose hospital shut down because of staffing shortages. The teacher whose classroom grew overcrowded with kids who don't speak English, while funding for education stayed flat. All betrayed. All abandoned.

Donald Trump's victories in 2016 and 2024 were fueled by his honesty about this crisis. He said out loud what millions already knew—that our borders were broken, that law and order were eroding, that leaders had abandoned their duty. Under Joe Biden, millions more surged in through caravans, and the crisis became undeniable.

In 2024, President Trump was right to call the southern border a disaster.

But it's also true today that walls and deportations alone cannot fix what is broken—not for the long term, and not without devastating consequences for the American economy. Mass deportation is not only cruel—it is impractical.

Just imagine: shelves emptied, houses half built—abandoned in the sun—restaurants shuttered, hospitals understaffed, entire industries collapsing overnight. That doesn't sound like the American Dream. It sounds like a nightmare. And that is what mass deportation would mean for the next three years.

Blanket amnesty (a free pass) for illegals, at the same time, is just as unreasonable and politically impossible. We are a nation of laws. A price must be paid. A free pass would send a message to the world: break our laws, and you win. Break our laws, and you can stay. Break our laws, and America rewards you. It would invite another wave of chaos, another wave of caravans, another betrayal of the American worker.

So what should we do?

We need a complete solution. One solution that works for President Trump, for Republicans, for Democrats, for the undocumented immigrants who have built their lives here, and for every American citizen who believes—rightly—that this is the greatest nation on earth.

One solution that secures the border *and* strengthens the American economy for good. (Quick note: President Trump passed $150 billion in *funding* for border security with his Big Beautiful Bill, but the *law* did not change. It could all disappear with the next administration, and the same border crisis we had in 2021, we could have again in 2028.)

One solution that ends illegal immigration forever *and* stabilizes the industries that feed us, house us, and entertain us.

One solution that gives dignity—not US citizenship—to people who have put down roots here, while requiring them to pay restitution to the country they entered illegally.

One solution that restores order, strengthens American workers, ensures this crisis is never repeated, and looks ahead to the jobs and industries that will sustain America's leadership for generations to come.

One solution that does what Washington has failed to do for forty years: bring courage, clarity, and finality to the most toxic and divisive issue of our time.

History has had mercy on us and put the right person at the White House. Donald Trump is the only leader who can deliver it. He is the boldest and most decisive president we've had in a century.

He has a once-in-a-generation opportunity: to solve this crisis once and for all, to secure America's future, and to restore confidence in our American system.

That solution is the **Dignity Act**, introduced in Congress in July 2025.

The Dignity Act offers legalization—not US citizenship. Let me repeat it again—not US citizenship, not amnesty, but stabilization for undocumented workers who have lived here at least five years. It secures the border, fixes asylum, invests in American workers, and adds trillions of dollars to our economy.

It lowers the costs of food for the average family and allows law enforcement officers to focus on the real criminals, the bad *hombres*, who happen to be those the president promised to deport en masse.

It is bold. It is final. It is revolutionary. It's Solomonic.

And I repeat: Donald Trump is the only one who can make it happen. President Trump could be for immigration what Abraham Lincoln was for slavery and what Ronald Reagan was for Communism.

How do I know? Because I have lived this story. I am the daughter of Cuban political refugees, born and raised in Miami. I grew up among immigrants, many of whom were illegal. As one of the founders of Univision, the most important Spanish television network in the country, I reported for thirty-five years on the reality that affects Hispanics in the United States. Today, in 2025, Hispanics are the largest minority in the United States—22 percent of the population.

As one of the most-watched Spanish-language journalists in America, this community was my audience. I was their storyteller and translator. I was their bridge. Long before I arrived in Congress in 2021, I knew them, and they knew me—very well.

But I was born in the United States, a first-generation American. So I also know the hard-working American who feels left behind. I know the family in Arkansas who got frustrated as they watched the caravans on TV. (I was yelling at my TV and shaking my head, too!)

I know the man in Youngstown, Ohio, who blames immigrants for crowded roads, rising housing prices, and lost jobs. His anger is real. His struggle is real. But his target is wrong. Deporting immigrants will not save him. It will not lower his mortgage, make his groceries more affordable, or secure his job. It will only make his life harder; he just doesn't know it . . . yet.

Who else? The young woman in Texas who worries that her children will never own a home because the system is broken. I know the retiree in Arizona who fears his Social Security will collapse under the weight of this chaos. I know the police officer in Florida who wonders why he spends his time looking for law-abiding families instead of hunting down gangs. All of them deserve the truth.

The truth has always been my North Star. As a TV journalist, I built my career on it. As a Congresswoman, I remain guided by it. And the truth is this: America's immigration system has been broken for forty years. Deporting everyone will not fix it. Amnesty—whatever that means—will not fix it. Only bold, final reform will fix it.

The mess has gotten bigger. Now, for the first time in forty years, Americans of every background are engaged on this topic. They are angry. They are demanding solutions. Immigration is no longer a crisis we can ignore.

We are standing at a crossroads. One path leads to cruelty, chaos, and decline. The other leads to order, prosperity, and renewal.

The United States has always striven to be a shining city on a hill—a place of refuge that attracts people like Albert Einstein—minds that will make us great. A place of second chances. Now is the time to remember that ambition and rise to it once again, with courage, honesty, and audacity.

Not with half-measures. Not with empty promises. Not with half-truths. But with the kind of resolve that built this country in the first place.

If we do, America will shine brighter than ever before.

That is the truth.

CHAPTER 1

It Won't Stop at the Criminals

- Politicians say deportations target "the bad guys," but to meet their target numbers, many "good guys" will get caught up in ICE raids and deported, too.
- A mass round-up will hurt farmworkers, construction crews, caregivers, and the average American more than it will hurt drug lords and traffickers.
- Real security means freeing ICE to focus on actual threats, not tearing apart communities.
- Without responsible reform, ordinary Americans will pay the price in higher costs, broken families, and unsafe streets.

FINDING THE BAD GUYS IS HARDER THAN FINDING THE GOOD GUYS

We are almost a year into President Trump's second term—and into his vow to "deport all the illegal criminals." What do we have to show for it? For some, fear, confusion, chaos. For others, someone is taking action—putting order in the House.

The headlines tell the story better than any speech. "Federal agents blast way into California home of woman and small children." "Small U.S. towns cancel fairs celebrating Latino culture: 'the climate of fear is real.'" "Chicago protesters defiant in face of President Trump's deportation threats." "Raid on upstate New York food manufacturer leads to dozens of detentions." "ICE arrests almost 500 people at Hyundai plant in Georgia." "Iranian woman, who has lived in the U.S. for 47 years, taken by ICE while gardening." "Dozens detained in U.S. immigration raids in New York state, governor says."

That doesn't mean criminals aren't being arrested. They most definitely are. And the headlines tell that side of the story, too. "Tens of thousands of illegal immigrants with sexual assault, murder convictions in US: ICE data." "Massive identity theft scheme led by illegal immigrants uncovered after raid at meatpacking plant." "DHS arrests five illegal immigrants convicted of serious crimes, including murder and child abuse."

But we must ask ourselves: Do you feel safer? Are we more hopeful about our future? Is this really what people voted for?

Here is another hard truth: it is costly, laborious, and difficult to find the worst illegal criminals. Criminals do not walk around with neon signs. They are smart; they are not cleaning buildings. They live in the shadows, too. We do not know who they are or where they sleep. We do not have enough agents to find, detain, and remove them fast enough to satisfy the arrest quotas imposed on the Department of Homeland Security (DHS) of around 3,000 illegals deported per day.

So to reach the numbers, the government is shifting the target.

Now, if ICE hits a home or workplace with a criminal target and finds five other illegals without a criminal record—an eighty-year-old grandmother who cleans homes, a father walking in from a night shift as a dishwasher, or a five-year-old in pajamas—they take them all. The strategy has a cold bureaucratic name—**collateral arrests—and it's a completely new policy.** In previous administrations, if an undocumented immigrant with a criminal record was apprehended, the system would process that person, deport them, and let the rest of the household go on with their lives. Not in 2025. Now they are taking illegals with no other criminal record.

The mission is to "get the numbers," and sometimes the easiest targets to seize are not the illegal criminals hiding in the dark corners—but the workers standing in the light. The factory hand whose foreman knows his name. The dairy crew at dawn. The woman who cleans rooms on the fourth floor. The usher at church. The moms at school pick-up. The righteous are being made to pay for the sinners.

If this continues for the next three years, the real-world consequences will be catastrophic for all of us. And it will be us— American citizens of all stripes—who will suffer most.

Let's be clear: these deportations are legal. The Trump administration is following the law. The statute says it plainly: anyone in the United States without lawful status is subject to removal. If an officer finds you and you cannot prove legal status, you can be deported. For decades, presidents of both parties recognized a practical truth: enforcing the law to a "T"—deporting every undocumented person—would harm the country. It would wreck local economies and crash key industries. So administration after administration used discretion. Justice and Homeland Security Departments wrote tailored rules, priorities, and memoranda. The mandate was to focus resources on genuine threats—meaning criminals. Even though it turned a blind eye to part of the law, there was a practical logic to it—protect the country while protecting the economy.

Then came 2025; Donald Trump broke with that modern consensus. He drew a line as bright as a sunrise: if you are here illegally, you are removable. Period. A clarifying statement in an era drowning in euphemism. People who had watched years of disorder at the border cheered. At last, a president saying what felt right. Specifically, in the last four years, those images of caravans and hundreds of thousands of people of all races, colors, and ages pouring into our country like a deluge.

But here is the disconnect—a gulf we rarely confront. The idea of "illegal immigration" is abstract. The lives of people are not. Many Americans simply do not know who their undocumented neighbors are, even when they see them every day, even when they hire them, even when they sit beside them in a pew. For undocumented families, status is a secret guarded like a wound. Shame and fear keep them in the shadows.

Understandably, people may support "deport them" in the abstract, but their reaction changes when the deportee has a name and a face and you happen to know them. It's a different feeling when it is the cashier who bags groceries at their neighborhood supermarket. Or when it is the neighbor who shovels their driveway every ice storm. Or when it is a friend or a coworker.

Not my guy.

This is the scenario now happening every day in America. In big cities, in small towns. Someone gets deported, and the average American is wondering what happened to Pepe. The text arrives: **Deported? Why him? He's a good man. He works hard. He's at church every week. I didn't even know he was undocumented.**

There it is, exposed in daylight: many people are okay with deportations—until it's *their* immigrant. Until it's *their* guy. Principle collides with proximity. Reality hits like a train.

THE INVISIBLES

These are the invisible people all around us, and they affect almost every aspect of your life.

Put yourself, for a moment, in the shoes of many ordinary Americans. I'll give some examples.

Getting a drink: You head to a bar with friends. Order a beer. The bartender might be a citizen. But who is changing the kegs, running racks through the washer? Before that IPA ever hit the tap—who picked the hops? Who processed the grain? Who drove the pallets to the brewery? At nearly every link, invisible hands you never meet.

Going to the salon: You plan a girls' weekend and stop for a manicure. The salon is immaculate; the service is kind, fast, and affordable. You know it is immigrant-owned. You assume they are all here legally. You only learn otherwise when ICE detains the owner—like Melissa Tran in Hagerstown, Maryland—who came from Vietnam as a child and built a small family business before being taken away in 2025.

An accident: You wake up in an ER after a crash. Doctors, nurses, PAs, and techs move like a single organism. In a nation short-staffed at every clinical level, odds are good that at least one person touching your care is foreign-born and, yes, some portion is undocumented. Without them, your wait lengthens, your outcome worsens.

It's Christmastime: You click "Buy Now." The package appears in two days. Who molded the parts? Who taped the box? Who sorted it at midnight and scanned it at 4:00 a.m.? You do not see them—but you rely on them.

A nice meal: You're in Omaha and order a steak with salad and mashed potatoes. That beef ran through a slaughterhouse—an industry that leans on immigrant labor like a spine. The lettuce and tomato likely came from fields in California or Florida, picked under the sun by people you will never meet. The Idaho potatoes traveled the interstates in a truck packed, loaded, and driven by men and women whose names you will never learn. One plate; dozens of anonymous hands. You don't see that you rely on them.

A birthday party: Your child turns five. You're at a local park. The grass is cut. Trash bins are empty. The pavilion swept. Who did it? The cake at the party is perfect. Who whisked the batter, iced the rosettes, and slid the box across the counter with a smile?

Sports practice: You drive to soccer practice. Sometimes you carpool. Then, one day, one of the moms is gone. It happened in Kennett, Missouri, to Carol Mayorga—twenty-one years in the United States, beloved in her community, a fixture at a local diner. "The most uplifting person you could hope to know," customers said. She went to what she thought was a routine ICE appointment. She left in shackles.

Church: You assume everyone at church is a citizen. Why wouldn't you? Yet one in twelve Christians in America is either at risk of deportation or lives in a household where someone is— Catholics and Evangelicals, pew by pew. Statistically, someone in your congregation is undocumented. You may not know who until the day an empty seat tells you.

In case after case, fear is an element of everyday life that can't be avoided.

The element of fear is palpable in every immigrant neighborhood across America. Illegals know that if the mission is numbers, enforcement cannot stop with "the criminals." It won't stop with collateral sweeps. It will move outward. To street corners at dawn, where crews looking for work gather. To factory gates; to kitchens; to school drop-off lanes. To the 2.6 million undocumented people married to American citizens, whose status cannot be adjusted under current law; to churches, to homes where the mortgage is paid, the taxes filed, and the young children pledge allegiance at school. For the kids, the only country they have ever known is the one now pushing them out the door.

If the administration truly pursues the promise to its end, we are not talking about a few raids. We are talking about mass arrests on a scale without precedent. A 2025 report by a coalition of faith groups estimated that as many as **ten million** Christians in the United States are either undocumented themselves or have a close family member at risk. A news outlet highlighted the core finding: **One in twelve of all Christians in America are personally at risk or in a mixed-status household.** Imagine the catastrophic consequences to faith communities—at a moment when religious affiliation is already falling, as quantified in a recent Pew Religious Landscape Study.

It would be the largest loss of religion in modern American history.

The bottom line is simple: immigrants—including those here without status—are stitched into the American fabric. They are in our economy, our congregations, our neighborhoods, our kitchens, our hospitals, and our fields. We can pretend otherwise, or we can choose a practical solution that serves the whole nation.

MASS DEPORTATIONS WILL DESTROY THE ECONOMY

Now let's zoom out and talk plainly about the industries that keep America alive—agriculture, construction, hospitality—and what happens if we pull the wrong thread.

You don't have to care about any one undocumented person's story to see the economic danger of mass deportations. Just look at the math of food. Roughly half of America's agricultural workforce is undocumented. Take those workers out on Monday, and you won't have food on your table by Friday. Not theory—logistics.

Planting, tending, and picking happen in windows you cannot extend. A missed harvest is not a delay; it is a loss. Agriculture is not only how we eat—it is a pillar of our exports. In the world, few countries can both feed themselves and sell to other nations. America is one of them. Undermine that, and you do not just raise prices; you shrink power at the global scale.

Remove that labor, and the shockwave races through the whole chain. Fields to packing houses. Refrigerated trucks to distribution hubs. Retail coolers to your dinner table. In the meantime, consumers are unforgiving, and supply chains are fragile. Lose the hands, lose the harvest. Lose the harvest, lose the margin. In a week, prices jump. In two, restaurant menus change. In three, your grocery list costs more than your budget.

That was agriculture, now let's talk about construction. Building, like farming, is carried on immigrant shoulders.

From the start, immigrants have been the backbone of America's ability to raise, to carve, to lift. Nearly everything that defines our landscape—from basic infrastructure to the marble pillars of our democracy—has immigrant fingerprints. The White House itself, and the Capitol dome. Yes, slaves were the primary builders of these early works. But alongside them were Scottish stonemasons, Irish carvers, and Italian artisans. The Capitol was modeled on the architecture of Rome and Athens, while Italian sculptors and painters crossed an ocean for their unmatched skill.

The Erie Canal. It connected our young nation; three hundred and fifty miles of earth and rock, dug by Irish hands, with Germans and Scots beside them. That channel became a gateway, tying New York to Lake Erie, to the Mississippi River, and to the West—unleashing commerce and settlement. Allowing us to grow as a nation.

The Transcontinental Railroad: a ribbon of steel hammered across desert and through mountains, nearly all by Chinese workers. Without it, there would be no continental connection, no industrial rise at the scale America achieved.

The skyscrapers and bridges of New York City—symbols that still awe the world—rose story by story on the backs of Irish, German, and Italian immigrants who balanced on beams, building four floors a week, while death waited below.

The Hoover Dam: Irish, Italian, and Mexican workers joined to pour the concrete and shape one of the twentieth century's wonders.

Even during World War II, when manpower thinned and priorities shifted, immigrants stepped into the breach. They kept factories humming, farms producing, bridges rising. America built because *immigrants* built.

Now ask: in 2025, what happens if we rip those hands out?

It's not just major infrastructure at stake. We are living through one of the worst housing crises in modern history. Prices skyrocket not only because of the cost of materials or zoning battles, but also because the country simply cannot keep up with demand. We are not building enough homes, for lack of labor, materials, and speed.

The Home Builders Institute, with the National Association of Home Builders, put the numbers down in black and white in June 2025. Even with the current workforce, legal or illegal, the labor is insufficient. Shortages alone are costing $10.8 billion every year—due to delays, to half-finished projects, and to production slowing by two months on average. Twenty thousand single-family homes a year we never build; that is billions in lost value, but more in lost dreams.

We cannot solve this crisis without more builders. We cannot increase supply without more workers. We cannot make homes affordable while deporting the very people swinging the hammers and laying the bricks.

Some claim deporting millions will free up housing—vacancies that will lower prices. It's a fantasy. Immigrants disproportionately live in cities, in crowded multigenerational households. The empty apartments left behind are not the single-family homes young families are desperate to buy. The idea that deportation would solve the housing crisis collapses on contact with the facts on the ground.

What deportation will do is stall construction even further. Fewer crews. Longer waits. Higher bids. Every American family already priced out of a mortgage will be pushed farther back. Home ownership—the heart of the American dream—drifts farther out of reach.

Mass deportations will not open the supply of homes. They would shrink it. They would deepen the crisis.

President Trump, a builder himself, knows this truth in his bones. He understands: if we lose our capacity to build, we lose our capacity to grow. Without builders, America stops rising.

There is a disconnect here: ICE's mandate does not pause for the housing market. After the criminals are gone, after the collateral is gone, the quotas remain. Who is next? The roofers. The drywall crews. The concrete finishers.

I explained where you live and what you eat. Let's talk about where you play.

Hospitality is no less vulnerable. Americans travel for business or for fun. We need hotels to stay in. We enjoy eating at restaurants. Our very way of life is built around service—and that service rests on immigrant hands. Legal and illegal, both. And even now, even with our current workforce, shortages are everywhere.

The James Beard Independent Restaurant Report in 2025 laid it out. Month after month, restaurants are short more than 200,000 workers. Hours cut. Doors closed a day a week for lack of workers. Ninety-one percent were forced to raise prices because of the wages needed to compete for scarce staff. Customers see it every time they eat out—the bill climbing, the wait longer, the service thinner.

At a recent stop at a popular South Florida sports bar and grill, I asked the owner to describe the challenges he was facing when it came to immigration and staffing. With fewer immigrants in the area—and workers afraid of getting picked up—he was struggling to find enough dishwashers to cover shifts. Dishwashers may be considered the lowest rung on the totem pole, he said, but they're a crucial cog in the restaurant's service. They set the tone for the entire kitchen. When dishes and glasses are dirty, waiters have to clean them themselves, adding extra pressure. Customers complain to the wait staff, even though it's not their fault—they're doing everything they can. Morale drops, dishes pile up, and the cycle spirals out of control.

What about your health and well-being?

The immigrant workforce touches all of us through healthcare. It touches caregiving. Immigrants are a pillar of medicine itself. Doctors, nurses, assistants, techs, janitors—immigrants at every station. Without them, ER waits stretch ten, twelve, sixteen hours. Clinics close earlier. Pharmacies reduce hours. Even basic services—an X-ray, a lab test—take days instead of hours.

Another fact of life: America is aging. Retirees surge. Caregivers are needed in every community. Who will tend the elderly when their own children are still in the workforce? Increasingly, it is immigrants—highly skilled, deeply compassionate, willing to step in to fill the gaps. If we deport en masse, we do not just lose field hands or roofers. We lose nurses. We lose aides. We will lose the caretakers who will one day tend to *us*.

During the pandemic, Americans learned what a supply chain was.

The ripple hits supply chains, too. Retail. Logistics. But the lesson is already fading. Immigrants have been filling those gaps—sorting in warehouses, driving trucks, delivering packages. And still, we fall short. The Niskanen Center study showed online retail shortages increasing from one out-of-stock item in 200 pages to one in fifty-nine pages. That is the standard dropping in real time. Fewer workers means slower fulfillment. Slower fulfillment means angry consumers and a lower quality of life. For employers, delays in the delivery of goods mean it's simply harder to do business.

Pharmacies, diners, shipping hubs—each one now shuts early or skips days. That is not an inconvenience. That is Americans losing access to food, to medicine, to paychecks. When FedEx slaps fees on deliveries because of labor gaps, when UPS extends shipping times, when USPS lengthens windows—it all falls on the customer. On you.

Still the demand grows. The labor force participation rate drops. Retirees increase. Elder care needs surge. Who will fill the breach? Deport the ones already here, and the breach becomes a canyon.

Even Federal Reserve Chairman Jerome Powell—cautious, careful Jerome Powell—was pressed to admit it under questioning in June 2025.

During a House Financial Services Committee hearing, I asked him straight: What is the effect of losing thousands of workers—"collateral damage"—in ICE's sweeps? At first, he hedged: immigration is not his lane, other agencies can make these types of projections, and the Fed takes immigration policy as it comes. But I pressed again, and he said it: "It [removing long-term workers] has obviously reduced the growth of the labor force. When you significantly slow the growth of the labor force, you slow the growth of the economy. I think growth will slow, and is slowing this year, and that is one of the reasons."

Straight from the horse's mouth, the Fed chair himself: deportations of good workers equal slower growth; slower economic growth means every American loses.

Here is a truth that most politicians won't say out loud: immigrants do the hard jobs most Americans will not.

How many citizens will pick oranges in the swampy heat of Florida? How many will spend hours under the California sun picking jalapeño peppers? These are brutal, backbreaking jobs. They always have been. Historically, those with the fewest choices filled them—be that building railroads across the desert, working in freezing slaughterhouses in the Midwest, or sweating on Alabama blueberry farms.

Immigrants are not stealing those jobs. They are filling them. They are complementary, not substitutes. By taking the lowest-rung work, they allow Americans to climb. They do not displace—they enable. Think about it this way: an immigrant in the field frees up an American citizen to work inside the air-conditioned warehouse. An American in the warehouse frees up another citizen to work in an administrative office. **A ladder can only be climbed if someone holds the bottom steady.**

Immigrants choose this work. No one forces them to harvest lettuce or wash dishes or clean hotel bathrooms. They choose it because, compared to where they came from, these jobs mean survival, progress, possibility. If the jobs weren't worth it, they would not cross deserts, risk swift rivers, or live under constant threat of deportation.

Immigrants are not only workers—they are consumers.

The National Immigration Forum put the number down: undocumented immigrants alone carried nearly **$300 billion** in purchasing power in 2023. Take them out of the economy, and you rip away billions in demand. Businesses collapse not only because they lose employees, but because they lose customers.

Every undocumented family buys food, clothes, gas, and diapers. Most undocumented workers pay rent, utilities, and phone bills. They go to sports games and concerts. Every paycheck they earn cycles back into the local economy.

Immigrants expand demand. They invest in neighborhoods. They open shops and rent storefronts. They are multiplier effects in human form. Deport them, and you contract the economy. Keep them, reform the system, and you expand it.

This is not charity. It is arithmetic. And because the economy touches everything, now, the American Dream hangs in the balance.

That dream has always been simple to say and possible to achieve: you can work, climb, save, buy, and hand your children something better. For two centuries, that promise was kept because the economy kept doubling—every twenty-five years, roughly, our wealth doubled. Immigration has always been part of that doubling. New workers, new consumers, new ideas. Growth compounded.

But today, for the first time in modern history, it is no longer guaranteed that children will be better off than their parents. And one of the biggest drivers of that slowdown is immigration policy—**both the illegal flow we refuse to fix and the legal system we refuse to modernize.**

If we shut the door, if we strip out millions who are already part of the machine, the American Dream dies. Not in theory. In practice. In paychecks and mortgages and empty shelves.

Again, we have a choice: invest in Americans, reform the system, raise the standard—or cling to slogans, deport the workforce, and watch the dream collapse within a generation.

FIX IMMIGRATION—DON'T WEAPONIZE IT

The current system satisfies no one. Immigrants live in fear, unsure if tomorrow brings a knock on the door. Citizens live in frustration, watching laws unenforced, chaos televised, and leaders impotent. Some demand mass deportation, believing a law broken must mean the harshest enforcement. Others plead for mercy, believing mercy, in this case, is an American value. Most simply want it solved—fairly, firmly, finally.

No political party created this mess. But Congress exists for one reason above all: to legislate when the people demand it. And we have a serious problem that needs a government response.

I have promised to tell the truth, and here it is:

- The system is broken.
- Deporting everyone will not fix it.
- A free pass to lawbreakers alone will not fix it.
- Only measured and practical reform can fix it.
- This reform must be firm, final, and enforceable.

Immigration is not a side issue. It is not a niche debate. It is the economy. It is national security. It reflects our values. It is the American Dream itself. Ignore that, and we imperil not only immigrants but the very future of this republic.

In administration after administration, presidents have kicked the can. Congress has failed to act. Both parties share the blame. But the American people are no longer content with paralysis. They are angry. They are afraid. They are demanding solutions.

We are at a crossroads. One path leads to collapse and decline. The other to reform, renewal, and the strongest America yet. The choice is ours. And a solution—the Dignity Act of 2025—was just introduced in Congress.

The truth is unavoidable: if America is to grow, to prosper, to keep its promise—immigration must be fixed, not weaponized.

CHAPTER 2

It's the Caravans, Stupid!

- The caravans that poured across the border under President Biden were a disaster—shifting the conversation from fixing the long-term undocumented to scrambling over short-term chaos. The urgent drowned out the important.
- An estimated 10–15 million people entered during Biden's term, from all over the world. They exploited an open border, while those who have lived and worked here for years are left paying the price.
- The chaos from these last four years made Americans less safe, and did a large disservice to the Hispanic community in America.
- Only the Dignity Act ensures we never face that kind of crisis again—restoring order, securing the border, and delivering a permanent fix.

BIDEN'S BORDER DISASTER
How did we get here—to such a dangerous place?

Biden. The caravans. It was an invasion right in front of our eyes.

For nearly four years, from 2021 to 2024, anyone tuning into television or reading a paper was met with horrifying images: caravans of men, women, and children moving north toward the southern border. Hundreds of thousands of people. Camps springing up along the way. Endless footage of people crossing rivers, clashing with border authorities, or simply walking past overwhelmed officers.

Again, the headlines painted the picture: "Biden admin has decriminalized and monetized chaos at the border: Kids are dying as a result of Biden's border 'experiment,' says the Arizona AG." "Migrant in potentially the largest caravan ever demands Biden keep asylum promise." The article went on: "The current number of close to 10,000 migrants is expected to swell to about 15,000 before it reaches the border . . . The caravan departed Tapachula on the Mexico-Guatemala border on Monday. The migrants, who mostly come from Venezuela, Cuba, and Nicaragua, will travel what is known as the coastal route to reach the U.S. border."

Fifteen thousand migrants? The numbers were staggering, and the visuals even more so—miles-long lines of people, tightly organized, seemingly supported by various networks and resources.

Fox drove the point home night after night: "Nearly 8,000-strong migrant caravan heads toward the US." "Migrant caravan demands Biden administration 'honors its commitments.'" "Migrant caravan containing thousands travels through Mexico toward US border: 'Tell Biden we are coming.'" "Growing caravan heads for US border in final months of Biden admin."

To most Republicans, the message from Biden to the world was obvious: *Come on in, everyone. The doors are open.*

The truth is, they were not entirely wrong. Early in 2021, President Biden halted new border wall construction. He reversed the "Remain in Mexico" program, which required asylum seekers to wait on the other side of the border while their cases were processed. That program, imperfect though it was, had discouraged fraudulent asylum claims. Its end signaled a shift.

Here is what President Biden did:

- He immediately revoked the border emergency.
- He stopped building the wall.
- He repealed seven executive orders that President Trump had in place, such as travel bans from dangerous countries.
- He supported the "U.S. Citizenship Act"—signaling he supported a guaranteed, easy, and quick path to citizenship for all illegals.
- He issued a "Root Causes" strategy to address "Migration from Central America."

Because of these actions, the perception among hopeful migrants around the globe was "you guys are welcome." Now it's the time to come in.

The most transcendental action was revoking the Title 42 border policy.

In May 2023, the administration ended Title 42—a Trump-era rule that allowed authorities to expel asylum seekers quickly on public health grounds during the pandemic. Removing that authority had predictable results. Crossings surged, reaching levels Americans had never seen before.

It was not just Venezuelans and Mexicans. Migrants came from China, Central Asia, Africa, and the Middle East. Criminals, human traffickers, and suspected terrorists were identified among them. The border was no longer a regional crisis. It was global.

Who were these people? Here are a few examples:

- 260,000 from India
- 190,000 from the Philippines
- 166,000 from China
- 124,000 from Russia
- 16,000 from Myanmar
- 15,000 from Mauritania
- 13,000 from Senegal
- 1,500 from Tajikistan

Why wasn't anyone stopping them? What kind of country simply lets millions of immigrants walk in—no questions asked? That's scary.

Biden's border policies, from a security perspective, were a joke—but by 2025, no one was laughing. Nothing like the southern border surge from 2021 to 2024 had ever happened before in US history. Many Americans, especially Republicans, saw it as an invasion.

The situation under Biden was lawless, reckless, and deeply irresponsible. It was terrible for the country in countless ways. But for Hispanics already living here, it was something else: a tragedy.

A FLOOD OF BIBLICAL PROPORTIONS

I came to Congress just as the Biden administration was turning the border into a full-blown crisis and a humanitarian nightmare. By early 2022, the wave of migration stretched from South America all the way to the United States.

I remember watching in disbelief as thousands upon thousands streamed in.

According to DHS data, just months into Biden's presidency, border encounters began breaking records. First 2,000 a day, then 3,000—nearly 90,000 a month. But it did not stop there. Crossings soon hit over 10,000 a day—250,000 a month. A quarter of a million. The system was buckling.

Over Biden's four years, more than 12 million people are estimated to have entered the country illegally, including 2 million known "gotaways"—individuals detected by surveillance but never apprehended. For the other 10 million, the story varied. Some were processed. Some were paroled in. Many were simply released with instructions to show up for a court hearing years later. *Catch and release*—allowing someone to come in while they are waiting for an asylum hearing that could be years away— became the operating standard. **It's the number one choice for illegals to game the system.**

People walked in by the thousands. Entire communities, especially border towns in Texas, Arizona, and New Mexico, were overwhelmed overnight.

But if that wasn't bad enough, let's talk about the children. Something very sinister was happening.

The system was so broken that then–Secretary of Homeland Security Alejandro Mayorkas admitted to me that authorities were unable to conduct DNA testing on hundreds of thousands of children brought across the border. Under Biden's policies, individuals arriving with a child or as part of a family unit were prioritized for quicker processing. The loophole was exploited. Adult men traveled with children who were not their own.

What happened to those children after entry remains mostly unknown. You can only imagine what that means. They most likely suffered the fate of all other human trafficking victims. We are still trying to account for what happened to them. Some were trafficked. Some were recycled—sent back only to be used again as another man's "child" on the next crossing.

By 2025, ICE could not locate 290,000 kids who they know entered the United States.

I am not exaggerating; this is the truth.

We—Americans—watched the crisis unfold with frustration and anger. We felt anger for the Border Patrol agents stretched beyond their limits, anger for Americans watching their laws flouted, and anger for the millions of undocumented immigrants who had lived here for decades, working, paying taxes, and raising families—who were suddenly buried under a new wave of chaos.

THE URGENT TAKES THE PLACE OF THE IMPORTANT

As the border became the white-hot center of the immigration debate, the national focus shifted entirely. It was no longer about the undocumented already here. It was no longer about Dreamers. It was no longer even about keeping families together.

It was about the border itself—irrespective of context. It was so bad that you could not talk about anything else.

Day after day, the caravans dominated the news cycle. Images of crowds pressing against fences, of children crying in overcrowded shelters, of overwhelmed towns declaring states of emergency—it consumed public attention. Immigration became synonymous with border failure.

But immigration is not just the southern border. The border is only one piece of a much bigger picture.

What Joe Biden did was the worst possible thing for the undocumented immigrants who had already built lives here. He undermined any chance at a serious national conversation. Long-time residents were pushed aside. The possibility of reform—already slim—was shelved indefinitely.

THE FORGOTTEN DREAMERS

Before Biden, immigration was deadlocked, but there was space for real discussion. DACA and the Dreamers—undocumented children brought here at a young age—were the focus of bipartisan sympathy.

Even many Republicans, who might oppose broader reform, had largely accepted Dreamers as "Americans in all but paperwork." At one point in 2018, President Trump himself was willing to strike a deal with Nancy Pelosi: $25 billion for border security in exchange for legal status for 1.8 million Dreamers. That was no small thing. It was proof that consensus was possible.

But politics got in the way. Think about it: President Trump was willing to give a path to citizenship to 1.8 MILLION Dreamers (first it was 800,000, then he took it to 1.8 million), and Nancy Pelosi, who's been crying and weeping about the poor kids, who you'd think would have done anything to make it happen, didn't go for it. No one really knows what happened, but I believe Nancy, who was the Speaker of the House at the time, could have negotiated something—if she really wanted to. However, politics prevailed. Words like "amnesty" and "wall funding" derailed the conversation and became poisonous. The deal collapsed. Then Biden came in and opened the border.

Public sympathy evaporated. The constant stream of images—caravans, border surges, stories of criminal activity—hardened public opinion. People saw millions arriving within a year and thought: *We are losing our country. This is un-American.*

The sequence became predictable: first deal with the new arrivals, then secure the border, then maybe—maybe—talk about Dreamers. Always pushed to the back of the line. Always "later."

By 2024, in the midst of a presidential election campaign, even the Biden administration was forced to reverse course. The numbers were too big. The chaos too obvious. Vice President Kamala

Harris, positioning herself for the presidency, publicly admitted the need for stronger border enforcement. She was supposed to be the Border Czar.

The confession was clear: the policy had failed.

But by then, the damage was done.

Between 2021 and 2024, Biden's border policy wasn't just a mistake. It was a betrayal of the Hispanic community. The American public started to turn on Latinos in a way I had never seen before.

It gave conservative pundits the moral high ground to argue for mass deportations. It gave Republicans political cover to pursue hardline policies. And it killed the conversation about anything else—Dreamers, DACA, long-time residents, reform.

The pendulum, having swung recklessly to the left, returned with equal force to the right.

THE LESSON ABOUT THE CARAVANS

This is the story of the caravans—four years of disaster. It is also the story of how leadership failed.

The border crisis did more than overwhelm towns and test agents. It reshaped the national debate. It turned sympathy into suspicion. It handed power to the most extreme voices. And it left millions of long-standing undocumented immigrants further in the shadows.

Congress has a lesson to learn here. Open borders are not compassion. Closed eyes are not leadership. When Washington fails to act, chaos fills the vacuum, and chaos always hurts the most vulnerable.

That is how we got here. And that is why we cannot afford to repeat the same mistakes again.

CHAPTER 3

The System Has Been Broken for Forty Years. And Guess What? It's Congress's Fault

- Since President Reagan last passed immigration reform forty years ago, both parties have allowed a crisis to brew and failed to address it. Both parties keep kicking the can down the road.
- Republicans demand border security but have been silent on broader immigration issues; Democrats overpromise on citizenship.
- Congress built a maze of loopholes and half-measures that encourage illegal entry. Congress has repeatedly failed to address this issue.
- Meanwhile, huge sectors of the economy have grown reliant on undocumented labor to stay competitive. This is wrong.
- Donald Trump changed the game. The border is secure but we are on a collision course with mass deportations.
- There is now an opening for practical reform.

WANDERING IN THE WILDERNESS

The immigration crisis did not begin with Joe Biden. It did not begin with the caravans. It did not even begin with Donald Trump or Barack Obama.

Biden was the straw that broke the camel's back. He took decades of unresolved tensions about who should be allowed into our country and in what numbers, and he poured gasoline on those embers until the fire raged out of control. When the flames spread, the Trump administration was the one left to quench the fire and try to put the house back together.

Immigration has been broken for a very long time. The last president to sign meaningful immigration reform was Ronald Reagan in 1986. Unfortunately, his reform failed so badly that we are still living with the consequences today.

In the last forty years, Congress has managed to take on and address nearly every other major national challenge—healthcare, infrastructure, environmental policy, tax reform. On immigration, we have failed at every turn. Every serious reform effort in Congress has collapsed.

For four decades, America has been wandering in the wilderness on immigration.

Why is it so intractable? Why is it so toxic? The answer begins with politics—plain, old-fashioned politics from both parties. For 250 years, politicians have toyed with immigration, using it to lure some voters while demonizing others, promising opportunity to one group while slamming the door on another. Immigration has always been a political football.

But the deeper truth is more damning: there are powerful disincentives to fixing immigration, and they trace back to a broken promise made by Ronald Reagan in 1986.

In the 1960s and 1970s, changes in US immigration law fueled a sharp increase in arrivals from Latin America. By the end of the

1970s, several million undocumented immigrants were already living here, working mostly in agriculture and other low-wage jobs that Americans would not take. As more economic migrants—especially from Mexico and Central America—continued arriving, pressure mounted on both parties to act.

So in 1986, Reagan did what presidents before him had done: he acknowledged the economic need for immigrant labor, while also recognizing the moral and logistical dilemma of millions of people living in the shadows. He advocated for and signed the Immigration Reform and Control Act of 1986, or IRCA—the last major immigration overhaul in US history.

Reagan's bill was, in essence, a deal with the American people: we will legalize those already here, and in return, we will enforce the law moving forward so we won't have illegal immigration ever again. In other words, we will seal the southern border.

The IRCA made it unlawful to knowingly hire illegal immigrants. At the same time, it legalized undocumented immigrants who had arrived before 1982. These included former guest workers, people who had overstayed temporary visas, and others who had crossed illegally. Nearly 3 million people—most of them Mexican—were placed on a path to citizenship. In exchange, the law promised strict penalties for employers who hired undocumented workers and serious new efforts to secure the border.

(The irony: nearly 70 percent of those 3 million did *not* take Reagan up on his offer for citizenship. They just accepted legal status to keep working, but did not pursue citizenship. Very few people know this. Why? It's what I've always said: The Hispanics don't necessarily want to be *gringos*. They just want a dignified life in the promised land. The same is true today.)

Reagan's idea seemed sound. Fix the problem, prevent it from spiraling, and move on.

At the time, Democrats and Republicans both considered it a fair compromise. Reagan passed the bill with bipartisan support. Millions of illegal immigrants gained legal status, a path to citizenship, and a chance to live openly in America.

But the second half of the deal—the enforcement—never came. Employer sanctions were ignored. Border security remained underfunded. The border itself was left porous and weak. I cannot stress this enough: this failure to deliver on border security and enforcement is the crux of the problem.

The result was predictable. More migrants kept coming—first in steady trickles, then in rising waves. Who could have guessed? Everyone, of course.

Many in Washington, especially Republicans, came to see Reagan's deal as a grave mistake. It had made the problem worse, not better. The failure to secure the border was a missed opportunity of historic proportions. What was once celebrated as reform soon became known—derisively—as "the Reagan Amnesty." For the record, Ronald Reagan is still revered in the Republican party, but he really screwed it up on immigration. (And ever since, "amnesty" has been the boogeyman—I'll get to it later.)

The fallout has lasted far beyond what Reagan could have imagined. To this day, Members of Congress recoil at any proposal that hints at large-scale legalization. My Republican colleagues in the House say it bluntly: "Reagan gave away citizenship, and we got nothing in return." To them, that lesson is seared into history. They are wary of walking down that road again.

They are not wrong to feel burned. But the blanket refusal to even reengage has become shortsighted, and dangerously so.

When Reagan's promise of enforcement collapsed, the system slid further into dysfunction. Then came the Clinton administration, which pursued border policies that—unintentionally—made matters worse. For years, immigrants had crossed back and forth across the border with the economic tides, coming north to work and then returning home. Much of the work was seasonal, and there were no real checkpoints at the border.

In 1994, Clinton initiated "Operation Gatekeeper" to try to stop border traffic. All of sudden, it made border crossings riskier, and increased the chance of not being able to get back in if you left. Ironically, instead of deterring undocumented migrants, it pushed many to stay permanently once they were here. In other words, families began separating, divided across the border.

By the early 2000s, illegal immigration had exploded into a full-blown crisis. President George W. Bush tried to restart the national conversation. But the terrorist attacks of September 11, 2001, shifted America's focus to national security, putting immigration reform on the shelf.

In his second term, Bush tried again. He negotiated with Mexican president Vicente Fox on something called "The Whole Enchilada." At one point, congressional Republicans pushed a bill that would have criminalized simply being present in the United States without legal status. The backlash was immediate and fierce. In response, lawmakers floated a different proposal that included a path to legalization. That bill passed the Senate—but died in the House.

Another opportunity for reform, gone.

By the mid-2000s, the verdict on immigration reform was grim. Burned once by Reagan, twice by Bush, the political right had given up. Immigration reform became a nonstarter.

In 2013, there was one more effort in Congress to do a comprehensive immigration reform bill: the Border Security, Economic Opportunity, and Immigration Modernization Act, what became known as the "Gang of Eight" bill for its group of sponsors. Four Republicans and four Democrats came together, an unlikely coalition in a time already defined by bitter partisan divides, and they tried to craft what looked, on paper, like a grand bargain. The bill included tougher border enforcement provisions, a mandatory E-Verify system for employers to ensure that new hires were legally authorized to work, and a thirteen-year path to citizenship for undocumented immigrants. It was rigorous, structured, and designed to assuage fears that citizenship would be immediate.

It was crafted by major figures from both sides of the aisle: John McCain, Marco Rubio, Lindsey Graham, Jeff Flake, Chuck Schumer, Bob Menendez, Dick Durbin, and Michael Bennet. It passed the Senate with sixty-eight votes—a landslide by modern standards—nearly 70 percent of senators, including a number of Republicans, signing on. And President Obama gave it his full-throated endorsement. For a brief moment, the impossible seemed possible.

But then something happened that would alter the trajectory of immigration politics in America for the next decade. Eric Cantor, the House Majority Leader—the second most powerful Republican in Congress at the time—lost his primary. He lost to Dave Brat, an economics professor who ran almost entirely on an anti-"amnesty" message.

Now, in Washington, those paying attention had one interpretation. Cantor wasn't back in his district enough. He had stopped showing up for the people who sent him to Congress. He was raising money for others, climbing the leadership ladder, not engaging in his congressional district, becoming another creature of Washington—the same story that has ended countless political careers before his. But the minute the dust settled, a different narrative took hold. Cantor had been talking openly about immigration reform. He had been considering bringing the Senate bill to the House floor. So when he lost, the anti-immigration groups pounced. They pointed to Cantor and declared: "He lost because of immigration."

It wasn't true. But the story stuck. Like we say in the world of television—perception is reality. It calcified into conventional wisdom. And suddenly, Cantor was no longer just another fallen majority leader. He was a warning sign, a cautionary tale, a canary in the coal mine for any Republican who thought about sticking his or her neck out on immigration.

The House of Representatives didn't even take up the Gang of Eight bill. Leadership wasn't going to risk it. Consultants whispered in closed-door meetings. Activists raised the alarm. "Don't touch immigration," they said. "Don't go near it. Do you want to be the next Eric Cantor?" Even longtime veterans of immigration policy—people who had devoted their careers to trying to find solutions—began quietly advising new members to stay away. "Don't waste your time. Don't waste your political capital. Immigration reform is where good intentions go to die."

And so the incentives became almost entirely negative. Why fight for a solution when all it would earn you was grief? Why put your name on the line when it might get you primaried, vilified, or worse? Better to stay quiet, stay safe, stay in office. Anyone who dared to try eventually walked away burned, muttering the same refrain: "I gave it a shot. I got hammered for it. It's not worth it. It's too hard."

This is how things stand **today.**

DEMOCRATS: OVERPROMISING AND UNDERDELIVERING

It isn't only Republicans who have failed to find a workable solution. In politics, there are always two sides to every coin. For years, Democrats have treated immigration like a political football—a tool to stir outrage, rally their base, and win votes, but never an issue they truly intend to solve. Where Republicans have mostly avoided conversation and steered clear of immigration reform

since Reagan and Bush, Democrats have consistently overprom-
ised to the Hispanic community with the too-good-to-be-true
message: *"Vote with us, and when we get into office, we will enact
major immigration reform—including an easy path to citizenship."*

And they have failed to deliver every single time.

They've had many chances. Between 2020 and 2022,
Democrats controlled the House, the Senate, and the White
House—a perfect trifecta. Speaker Nancy Pelosi, one of the most
powerful figures in modern American politics, moved massive
infrastructure spending, COVID relief, gun legislation, and environmental reform. She knew how to push through major legislation when she wanted to. Yet even with the gavel in her hand, she
never brought immigration reform up for a vote—not even the
Biden-endorsed U.S. Citizenship Act.

Why? Because, politically, many Democrats think it's more
valuable to keep the issue alive than to actually solve it. It has
been that way for years. Always promises. Never action.

I remember it clearly. In 2008, as a reporter, I was in the room
when President Barack Obama looked Univision's Jorge Ramos
in the eye during a widely broadcast interview and promised comprehensive immigration reform. As a Spanish television network
anchor, I will never forget it. "I cannot guarantee that it is going
to be in the first 100 days," Obama said. "But what I can guarantee is that we will have in the first year an immigration bill that I
strongly support and that I'm promoting. And I want to move that
forward as quickly as possible."

Among Hispanic communities, it became known as *Obama's
Promise*.

And with a supermajority—sixty votes in the Senate and
control of the House—it seemed Obama might finally be the
Democrat to deliver. The rules of Congress all but guarantee that
any serious attempt at immigration reform must be bipartisan. In

the Senate, debate cannot even begin unless sixty senators agree. But with sixty Democratic senators, Obama had a rare opening. Nothing stood in his way.

Yet when the moment came, he chose to spend all his political capital on the Affordable Care Act. Obamacare passed. But the aftermath cost Democrats the House of Representatives, and with it, their trifecta. Immigration reform died on the vine. Once again, the can was kicked down the road.

So despite their promises and despite a once-in-a-lifetime supermajority, President Obama, Vice President Biden, and the Democratic Party chose other priorities. In the 2010 midterms, the Tea Party wave swept Republicans into the House, giving them a historic majority in 2011 to confront Obama's legislative agenda for the rest of his presidency. The Senate was still blue, but with fewer than sixty votes. The House was red. Congress ground to a halt.

Now, some will point to the budget reconciliation process—the one loophole to the sixty-vote rule in the Senate. Reconciliation allows certain budget-related bills to pass with just fifty votes. Republicans used it in 2017 and again in 2025 for tax cuts. Democrats used it under Biden for COVID relief and a green energy bill. But reconciliation has strict limits. The Senate parliamentarian—the nonpartisan rule-keeper—has already ruled that legalizing immigrants does not qualify. In other words, immigration reform cannot be done through reconciliation. It has to be done the old-fashioned way. There is no fast track. There is no partisan shortcut. Without sixty votes from one party in the Senate, you need bipartisanship. Period.

Facing a divided Congress, Obama turned to unilateral executive action. In 2012, he created DACA—Deferred Action for Childhood Arrivals. It was meant to protect certain undocumented immigrants brought here as children, the Dreamers, from deportation. Republicans called it illegal. They argued immigration policy could not be written by executive order, and that the president lacked the authority to enact such sweeping changes without Congress. Obama called it temporary—a bridge until lawmakers delivered a permanent solution. But more than a decade later, it remains in place. Renewed every two years, but closed to new applicants. At its peak, over 700,000 Dreamers were enrolled. Today, closer to 500,000 remain, as others left, shifted status, or fell through the cracks. We have no idea how many were eligible and never applied.

Still today, uncertainty hangs over every Dreamer's head. Courts continue to debate its legality. States like Texas keep filing lawsuits to dismantle it. The president could revoke it with the stroke of a pen. Every two years, renewals come with dread. It is a fragile existence. A life lived on borrowed time.

Here is the bitter irony. Before and after DACA, the Obama administration deported more people per year than any other president in recent history—more than Bush, more than Biden, more than President Trump. He earned a nickname that cut deep in immigrant communities: *the Deporter in Chief*. Business owners felt the sting when his agents raided worksites. Families felt it when their fathers, mothers, and children were torn away.

This was the Democratic record: promises made, promises broken, and lives left in limbo. And the legacy media, silent. Why? Because we're talking about the Deporter in Chief himself, President Obama. He was never accused, never held accountable in the public square, but this is where the Democrats started to lose the trust of the Hispanics.

TRUMP CHANGES THE GAME

Donald Trump enters the scene: a construction mogul from New York who wants to be president. In fact, he detonates it. He picked up the political third rail of immigration and wielded it like a sword. He did what no Republican before him had dared: he made immigration the centerpiece of his campaign, a signature issue of his politics.

In 2014, Republicans retook the Senate. In 2016, President Trump stormed into the White House by promising to "build the wall," to ban travel from countries he declared dangerous, and to put America first by stopping what he characterized as an uncontrolled flood of illegal immigration. His words were blunt, but they resonated deeply with millions of voters who felt abandoned, ignored, left behind.

By the end of Obama's second term, Americans were already restless, asking: "We are the most powerful country in the world. Why can't we secure our border? Why is our immigration system still so broken? Why are there so many illegals here? Can't we do something about it?" The questions were there, lingering in town halls and kitchen tables. But until Trump, no national leader had grabbed them and blasted them into the center of the national stage.

Trump did that. And when he did, immigration shifted overnight from a neglected problem to the single hottest flashpoint in American politics. But remember, immigration is not just border security. I repeat, immigration is not just about border security.

His message was clear and cutting: "We have a problem. Illegal immigrants are here committing crimes. The border is a sieve. We have to secure it." That message landed. It spread. And combined with the growing perception—particularly in white, working-class America—that the country was being overwhelmed, that its cultural and economic fabric was being strained, it transformed the Republican Party's posture. Immigration was no longer an issue you avoided. It was the issue you ran on. But I repeat, border security is just one aspect of immigration.

Trump redefined it as a litmus test. And suddenly, the boundaries of Republican politics snapped into place: you could talk about immigration, but only if you talked about it the Trump way. Hardline. No compromise. No legalization. Just walls, and enforcement.

MARIA COMES TO WASHINGTON

"I'm coming to Washington to fix immigration," I told my inner circle in December 2020, fresh off my first congressional win.

Immigration wasn't just another issue for me—it was the issue. I was uniquely positioned, knowledgeable, and willing to speak truths others dodged. What I did not yet know was just how hard the fight would be.

We were gathered at the Capitol Hill Hotel, huddled around a scratched table, plotting out my first term. You could almost feel the oxygen leave the room as soon as the words crossed my lips.

"What?!" one of them blurted.

"Why would you do that?" another asked, shaking their head.

Their counsel was swift and unanimous: Immigration reform was toxic. It was the graveyard of political careers. People had tried for thirty-five years and failed. "Remember Eric Cantor," they said. "Remember the Gang of Eight in 2013. Immigration is a trap. Everyone who touches it ends up burned."

"That's what I'm going to do," I told them anyway.

Just a few weeks earlier, on November 5, 2020, I had pulled off one of the most stunning political upsets in the nation.

Against every prediction, in defiance of the polls and the pundits, I flipped Florida's 27th congressional district. I unseated Donna Shalala, the longest-serving member of the Clinton cabinet. She had been the president of the Clinton Foundation, and was a personal friend of Bill, Hillary, and Nancy Pelosi. Shalala had defeated me in 2018 when Florida District 27 was an open seat. She was a powerful and well-funded incumbent member sitting in a district Joe Biden had carried by over three points. (Thinking about it now, it was really a miracle.) With zero financial help from the Republican establishment—I did my own fundraising—I unseated Shalala by 2.8 percentage points. It wasn't just a win—it was a political earthquake. *Politico* labeled it as the biggest upset in the country that year. (Praise the Lord, but be careful what you wish for.)

"You just won the toughest race I've ever seen in my life," one of my advisors said. "And now you want to risk it all on immigration? You have such a great future in the Republican Party. Why would you want to blow that up?"

I knew my mission. It was immigration.

The warnings only grew louder. Every time I whispered the word "immigration" to someone on my team, I heard the same message repeated back to me: Don't touch it. It's radioactive. The timing is wrong. The politics are hopeless. Each side is too entrenched. And I was a freshman congresswoman with no political capital, no allies, no donor network, and no seasoned staff to back me up. They were right about the odds. But I wasn't a career politician. I didn't calculate based on fear. This was a problem that demanded a solution, and Congress existed to solve problems. I knew the solution. I was Hispanic. That was my job now.

"Do immigration, and you'll be a one-term congresswoman," they said.

"So be it," I thought.

I was going through orientation while this conversation was happening. I didn't know how to be a Congresswoman. I had never served in local government or the state legislature, like most Members of Congress, to give me a foundation for lawmaking and government service. It was a lot to learn and take in. There was a whole revolution going on in my head.

At the same time, I was hiring staff. That's when John Mark showed up. He was one of the first people I interviewed. He came recommended by my chief of staff, who had worked with him on environmental issues when John Mark was at the EPA. I asked him directly about immigration the first time we met. His answer has stayed with me ever since.

"Someone needs to tackle this," he said. "No one has the guts. But if you care about it, you should be the one, and I will help you."

He didn't flinch. He didn't warn me away. He leaned into the fight. He talked about the stakes, the human impact, and the national security risks of a broken system. He told me he had always carried a passion for helping people, that he wanted to change the world for the better.

Fixing immigration, he argued, wasn't just the right thing to do as Americans, or as Christians, or as Hispanics in positions of leadership. It was the responsible thing to do for the future of our country. I hired him on the spot. Now, five years later, he is the driving force behind this legislation and one of the two most deserving people to receive the dedication of this book.

From that moment on, we went to work. (We haven't stopped ever since.) We started building the bill from scratch. I set the vision, laid out my principles—border security, asylum reform, dignity to the millions already here, and a framework strong enough to win support in Congress.

By March 2021, just three months into my first term, I announced my intention to introduce the Dignity Bill. "No political party holds a monopoly on compassion," I said at the press conference. "The principles in my plan will bring dignity to the undocumented while we secure our border. We have a crisis on the southern border. Children are being trafficked. Families

are at risk. It is time to fix our broken system once and for all."
Remember, border security is not immigration.

Most people barely blinked. Another freshman with a flashy
idea. Another press conference destined to fade into the background noise of Washington. Everyone had seen it before—big
promises that died in committee, or in leadership's office, or in the
unforgiving glare of cable news.

And to make matters harder, we had to write the bill in semi-se-
cret. Immigration fell under the House Judiciary Committee, and
neither the chair nor the subcommittee leaders wanted anything
to do with immigration reform at the time. If I had gone to them
for support, they would have shut me down instantly. It wasn't
personal. They simply had their own priorities, and mine wasn't
one of them.

They wouldn't have given me staff or resources. More likely,
they would have buried the bill before it ever saw daylight.

Normally, drafting a bill of this size—250 pages—means rely-
ing on teams of lawyers, legislative experts, and committee staff
to translate vision into precise legal language. Without that infrastructure, it was just John Mark and me. He wasn't a lawyer, but he
knew immigration policy better than anyone I'd met. He became
my architect, building the scaffolding of a several-hundred-page
bill from the ground up, grinding late nights and weekends, poring
over language, hammering out details.

By early 2022, after a year of back-and-forth, we had it: a fully
developed immigration reform package. Sweeping. Serious. Ready
for Congress.

In February 2022, we introduced the first version of the Dignity
Act. It was official. It was filed. Every Member of Congress had it
in their hands. We were no longer talking about ideas. We had
put forward a blueprint for action.

I was proud. We had done what few believed possible: produced a real plan, detailed and defensible, to confront the immigration crisis head-on. But I also knew the introduction was only the beginning. Drafting is one thing. Passing is another. The hard work—building trust, creating coalitions, winning hearts, and breaking through decades of entrenched resistance—was only just beginning.

Because in Congress, nothing moves without trust. And on immigration, trust was broken.

THE BREAKDOWN OF TRUST

Congress only acts when the pain becomes unbearable. And even then, it usually waits until the last possible moment to move. If a system is limping along, Washington will always find a shinier crisis to chase.

Immigration has suffered most from this dysfunction. And the truth is simple: the only way to pass serious legislation outside of budget reconciliation is through compromise. Compromise requires trust. On immigration, trust does not exist. And fear is abundant. Fear. Fear. Fear.

After Reagan's failed deal, Republicans simply do not believe Democrats will ever follow through on securing the border once they have given some type of legalization to those here illegally. Democrats, hardened by President Trump's unapologetic stance, do not believe Republicans will never grant permission for the undocumented immigrants to come out of the shadows—even if the border is ironclad. The result is paralysis.

But here's the fact: border security is not immigration. Immigration is not border security. They are linked, but they are not the same thing.

President Trump proved you can secure the border. He did it within his first 100 days. The chaos at the border ended. The southern frontier was locked down. The caravans stopped. The crisis at the gates was contained. The border was at peace.

On top of that, on July 4, 2025, he signed the One Big Beautiful Bill Act—a working families tax cut bill that also poured $150 billion into border enforcement and immigration control.

President Trump's One Big Beautiful Bill Act gave us the first real opening to address this issue in years. Enough time has passed since the last collapse of an immigration deal. Republicans finally got the investment in security they have wanted. And now the conversation is shifting. Immigration is back at the top of the agenda. It dominates the news. It fills the airwaves. It fuels arguments at kitchen tables.

Now the question is not about the border. It is about the people already here. It is about the workforce. It is about the American economy and the American future.

Still, the structural reality remains. Unless one party manages to win sixty seats in the Senate—a political near impossibility in a divided nation—immigration reform must be bipartisan. That means both sides will have to sit down, swallow their pride, and strike a deal. There is no other path.

Yes, the border is calm, but ICE raids and mass deportations are causing new problems. Employers are sounding the alarms. Americans are starting to see communities fractured. Immigrant families live under constant dread. Immigration, in some form, remains a front-page story every single day.

And what the administration is doing now is dialing up the temperate on the pressure cooker. The country is straining. Many are demanding a reasonable solution.

If we do not solve this crisis soon, the costs will be devastating—human, economic, and political. Immigration reform, long dismissed as a luxury, is no longer a "want." It is a national necessity.

Chapter 4

Dignity—A New Proposal for Immigration Reform

- Dignity is a bipartisan solution; the *only* bipartisan immigration solution.
- The Dignity Act permanently secures the border and stops illegal immigration, while allowing long-term, contributing immigrants to come out of the shadows.
- Dignity requires restitution, accountability, and lawful participation—but no path to citizenship.
- Dignity participants pay $7,000 spread over seven years plus an additional 1 percent levy out of every paycheck.
- Dignity makes E-Verify mandatory.
- It only applies to immigrants who have been here five years or more (before 2021). They must pass a strict background check.
- They cannot receive federal benefits and must purchase their own health insurance.
- Dignity is tough, fair, and permanent—a onetime fix that ends the cycle. You can go home for Christmas. You won't be deported.

A BIPARTISAN PATH

In Washington today, compromise has become a dirty word.

It is treated almost like a betrayal—finding middle ground means surrender. Our politics mirror a deeply divided nation. Presidential elections are decided by a few thousand votes in a handful of swing states. Everyone has a strong opinion about everything—each side convinced they are right, while the other side is dangerously wrong.

Immigration is no exception. It is one of the most divisive, emotional, and stubborn issues in our national conversation. And that is exactly why it is also one of the most difficult to solve.

There is no silver-bullet argument. No one perspective carries the whole truth. Any honest attempt at a solution requires acknowledging that immigration looks different in every corner of the country.

In Congress, there are 435 districts, each with about 750,000 people, and every representative sees the problem through the lens of the people they serve. An agricultural district sees immigration through the prism of farming and labor. A border district sees it through security. A dense urban district sees it through the human impact—the neighbor, the co-worker, the friend who lives in the shadows.

Each view is valid in its own context. But each view is incomplete. It is natural for people to focus on the part that affects them most. If you are worried about cartel violence on the border, you are not thinking about berry fields in California. If you are worried about who is picking those berries, you are not thinking about how asylum policy affects Texas. To solve immigration, we have to see the whole picture. It is like a chain of dominoes—push one piece, and half a dozen others fall.

That is why bipartisanship is not a luxury; it is a necessity. You cannot pass immigration reform with one party or one region forcing its will on the rest of the country. You have to walk people through the problem, show them where past attempts have failed, point out where common ground exists, and explain how each piece fits together.

Any serious reform must work in a border town, in a farm community, in a tech hub, and on the factory floor. It must speak to Republicans and Democrats alike. And that is why, when it comes to immigration, the real question is not "who's right and who's wrong?" but "what does each side get right, and how do we build from there?"

THE DIGNITY ACT

The world has changed dramatically in the five years since I was elected to Congress in 2020—and in the three years since we first introduced the Dignity Act. A global pandemic that upended lives and economies. The Biden presidency, with its chaos at the border. Wars in Ukraine and the Middle East. And then Donald Trump's extraordinary comeback and reelection, reshaping American politics yet again.

Meanwhile, the immigration crisis has not stood still. It has grown more urgent, more pressing, and more impossible to ignore.

The Dignity Act has evolved too. The version we introduced in July 2025 is not the same bill I brought forward in my first term in Congress. It reflects hundreds of conversations—with border sheriffs, mayors, farmers, business owners, union leaders, independents, Democrats, Republicans, and, most importantly, immigrants themselves. I have listened. I have argued. I have sought compromise where compromise seemed impossible.

The Dignity Act of 2025 is the product of those disagreements, those debates, and those tough choices. It is a carefully crafted solution to meet the current circumstances. And while it cannot be the perfect solution for everyone, it is the most practical, most durable, and most American path forward that we have seen in forty years.

At the center of this vision is an answer to the question no one has had the courage to answer honestly: What do we do about the millions of undocumented immigrants who have lived in this country for five, ten, even twenty years? These are not the people who surged through Biden's wide-open border. These are not the lawless gangs like Tren de Aragua or the newly arrived caravans. These are the long-term residents who have worked, raised families, paid taxes, and lived quietly among us—yet have remained trapped in the shadows of illegality.

I call them the "contributors." I believe they are the key to solving the crisis once and for all.

Dignity is not designed to reward undocumented immigrants. Its purpose is to do what is best for Americans. And by doing so, it improves the lives of those living in the shadows as a byproduct. The aim is to stabilize industries, lower costs for consumers, secure our border forever, and give law enforcement the ability to focus on criminals instead of workers. In short, it is about restoring order, fairness, and strength to our immigration system in a way that serves every American.

Here is the topline: The Dignity Act provides a reasonable and final solution to America's immigration crisis. It ends illegal immigration to the United States once and for all, reestablishes law and order, provides a practical solution for the long-term undocumented, revitalizes the American workforce, and restores America's economy. In other words, it makes America greater.

Key Points of the Dignity Bill

- No path to citizenship
- Secures the southern border
- Mandates E-Verify

- Reforms the asylum system (stops catch and release)
- Protects Dreamers
- Imposes stiffer penalties on child sex traffickers
- Brings in $50 billion in revenue to the Treasury to pay down our debt
- Invests $70 billion in job training and apprenticeships for American workers
- Creates humanitarian campuses to quickly process asylum seekers
- Creates a new "Dignity status"—not a green card as we know it today—for long-term contributors who have been here more than five years
- Grows America's economy by improving our legal immigration system
- Ensures American competitiveness around the globe

The Dignity Act begins where all real reform must begin: with border security. The bill will codify strong, permanent enforcement that no future president can undo. In other words, border security is now set in stone by Congress, so it cannot be changed at the whim of any future president.

Securing the Border

It installs enhanced physical barriers where they are needed, deploys the most advanced surveillance technology, and provides the manpower to monitor it all—and shut down all illegal crossings.

A true fix is multilayer, and it must go beyond traditional border security. The border is just the first line of defense. The Dignity Act raises penalties for illegal crossings and imposes the toughest punishments in American history for child sex traffickers. It even introduces DNA testing to prevent fraudulent family claims. Together, these provisions do what every other immigration bill has failed to do: they ensure illegal immigration cannot happen again.

Fixing the Asylum System

Ever heard of catch and release? The bill kills it. Under current law, migrants can cross the border, claim asylum, and be released into the country while they await a hearing—sometimes years away. This "catch and release" policy has been a magnet for abuse. The Dignity Act ends it. No asylum seeker will be released into the United States until their claim has been decided. To make this possible, the bill establishes at least three new humanitarian campuses near the border, where asylum cases are processed within sixty days. They cannot leave the campus until we determine their fate. Humanitarian campuses are a new concept we created, a bipartisan compromise I worked out for swift asylum decisions.

This preserves due process and restores order. No more gaming the system. No more endless waiting. No more walk-ins. You wait with your family until the US authorities tell you you are welcome or you have to go back home. The best part is that it only takes two months.

It's Dignity, Not Amnesty

The real revolution of the Dignity Act is the Dignity program itself.

It's Dignity, not amnesty. No path to citizenship ever.

Let me be clear: this is not amnesty. (Whatever amnesty means, since everyone has a different definition.) There are no tricks—no citizenship. No one becomes a gringo.

The Dignity program creates an earned opportunity to stay in the country. Dignity does not offer US citizenship. It only applies to undocumented immigrants who have been living in the United States for five years or more.

It does not apply to those who entered under Biden's caravans. We cannot and will not fix the failures of that administration. But those who have lived here for years before Biden got to the White House, who have built lives, worked jobs, raised families—they should not be punished for the new wave of immigrants that overwhelmed our system.

To qualify, applicants must clear a strict criminal background check. They must prove they have lived here for more than five years. They must show a history of work and productivity. In other words, they must prove they are safe, stable, and contributing members of society to distinguish between the surge and the long-term undocumented.

Some people are saying that I am cruel. But we must draw a line. A hard line. There is a world of difference between the surge of illegal crossings that came under Joe Biden's open-border policies and the millions of undocumented immigrants who have been here for years, even decades.

The Dignity program makes that distinction crystal clear.

A Onetime Deal

Yes, it's a one-shot deal—available only to those who were already here before December 31, 2020. No excuses, no loopholes. Join now or lose your chance.

For these long-term undocumented residents—the contributors—the program offers something new: a chance to come out of the shadows, work openly, buy homes, open bank accounts, have a credit card, pay taxes, and go home for Christmas or to bury your mother.

Now to the fines: Each participant will pay $7,000 in restitution, spread over seven years.

The conditions are strict. Applicants must comply with all state and federal laws. They must begin paying all federal and state income taxes according to their tax bracket the moment they are enrolled in the program.

Now to the salary: They will pay an additional 1 percent levy out of every paycheck.

No federal benefits: Participants in the Dignity program can receive no entitlements. No benefits. No shortcuts. Dignity participants will not receive federal aid of any kind. They must also buy their own health insurance, so they are no longer a burden on our healthcare system. (The 1986 Emergency Medical Treatment and Labor Act—EMTALA—requires emergency rooms to treat people, regardless of their ability to pay, or their legal status. The costs of this are enormous. In 2024, for example, Florida spent $660 million on health care for illegal immigrants, a figure that includes nearly 70,000 emergency room visits.)

Contrary to what detractors would say, instead of taking from American taxpayers, they will become net contributors—both to the tax base and to the strength of the US economy.

The Dignity program lasts seven years. During this time, they must check in with DHS regularly and remain in good public standing. If they complete all the requirements and pay all the fines by the end of the seven years, then they complete the Dignity program.

After that, they can receive the "Dignity status" which allows them to stay in the country and keep working for seven more years. They can keep renewing this indefinitely. They remain ineligible for citizenship or benefits with the Dignity status, but it will allow them to stay and work as long as they want, assuming they maintain good behavior and do not commit any crimes. Otherwise, their status is ended and they will be deported.

A Big Pot of Money for the US Economy . . .

For any American worker who feels that an immigrant has taken their job or taken an opportunity from them, good news: we will provide you the opportunity to learn a new skill, or to do something different than what you were doing before. The more you learn, the more you earn.

Their $7,000 restitution payments, pooled together, will create a $70 billion fund dedicated to training and upskilling American workers—ensuring our citizens are ready for the best and most competitive jobs of the future. This money will be distributed to states to use for the most in-demand careers.

Dignity allows American workers to tap into new funds, paid for by immigrants, and expand their skills and job options.

This would be an estimated $70 billion from the $7,000 payments, going directly to American workers. It will be the single largest investment in the American workforce in modern history. Those funds will build apprenticeships, workforce training programs, and new pathways for education. For every undocumented immigrant who participates in the Dignity program, at least one American worker can be trained or retrained for an in-demand job. That is not theory—that is baked into the structure of the program.

But that's not all. Their 1 percent levy on their yearly salary will generate at least $50 billion to pay down the national debt.

. . . At No Cost to Taxpayers

Another pot of money comes from the 1 percent payroll levy. That revenue pays for the administration of the program itself and then flows straight into reducing the national debt—an estimated $50 billion. Republicans have long demanded fiscal discipline. For the first time, here is a program that delivers it without raising taxes on American citizens.

The Dignity program will not cost the US taxpayers one penny. All of it—not paid for by American taxpayers, but by the very undocumented workers seeking to remain in America. That is the essence of fairness. That is the essence of accountability. Nothing like this has ever been proposed in the history of this country.

It's steep and fair.

WHAT ELSE IS IN THE BILL?

I don't want to bore you with the details. But there are a few other provisions worth mentioning:

- **Trade and Commerce:** The Dignity Act improves our ports of entry at the border, increasing legal trade commerce. It expands inspection lanes and invests in X-ray technology to safely and quickly inspect commercial vehicles. These are so large that an eighteen-wheeler truck can drive through them, and we can see everything inside. With these, it's no longer possible to hide people or drugs inside. It's a game-changer for stopping fentanyl. Also, goods from Mexico and Canada can come in quicker and not be delayed by long waits at the border. (No more delays on trucks full of avocados, Coronas, or Modelos.)
- **Cartel Spotters and Repeat Border Jumpers:** The Dignity Act severely increases penalties for people who have already crossed the border. If you try again, you are going to jail. Zero tolerance moving forward.
- It also goes on the offensive against the cartels. On the Mexico side of the border, cartel spotters often track the

movements of border patrol so they can find the right places and times to sneak people and drugs across the border. We couldn't do anything about them—until now. The Dignity Act makes tracking border patrol movements (spotting) a crime and allows US personnel to go after them. It also makes it a crime to destroy any sensors on the border that help detect illegal crossings.

- **American Families United:** The Dignity Act includes the American Families United Act, which allows mixed-status families to stay together. Did you know that over 2.5 million Americans have undocumented spouses? They are currently at risk of separation or deportation. This policy allows them to stay together, which puts the interests of the American citizens first. Therefore, the Dignity Act benefits US citizens, promotes family unity, and prioritizes keeping families together.

DIGNITY IS THE RIGHT WAY FORWARD

Two things are true about the United States of America. We are a nation of laws. And we are a nation of second chances.

Ephesians 4:32 says, "Be kind to one another, tenderhearted, forgiving each other, just as God in Christ has forgiven you."

So the question becomes: how do we reconcile these truths in the immigration debate? The answer begins with an honest conversation—between Democrats and Republicans, between immigrants and citizens, between the undocumented and law enforcement, and most of all, between the American people themselves.

The hardliners on my right will insist: "A crime is a crime. Whether you killed someone or crossed the border illegally, you broke the law. You are a criminal just by being here."

But that argument ignores a crucial fact. Our legal system does not treat every violation the same way. Nor should it.

There is a world of difference between driving 120 miles an hour down a highway and going ten miles over the limit. One will land you in jail. The other will earn you a fine, maybe a warning. The nuance matters.

Did you know that crossing the border without authorization is not, under current law, a criminal act? It is a civil offense. Civil offenses are handled differently from other crimes. They are not about punishing the offender; they are about resolving disputes. That is why immigration cases are processed through civil proceedings—deportations, hearings—rather than criminal trials.

The distinction matters because under the Dignity program, the first step is not denial. It is a confession. Any undocumented immigrant who wants Dignity status must sign a document admitting the truth: "I entered this country illegally." That is an admission of guilt, but not of criminality.

This is the starting point of accountability.

Too often, Americans speak past each other on immigration because we are armed with different sets of facts, different assumptions, and different fears. But here is what I believe: every human being falls short. We are all sinners, in one way or another.

So we must ask: is the "sin" of coming to America—the desire to work, to provide for family, to seek a better life—so grave that it deserves the harshest punishment of deportation? Or can we offer a second chance to those who have proven, year after year, that they are not a burden, but a part of our fabric and have fulfilled a necessity in our marketplace?

I believe we can. I believe we must. Not just because it is merciful, but because it is wise.

For forty years, our nation has stumbled through half-measures and broken promises. Dignity is designed to be the final fix. A onetime deal. A covenant between the American people and the millions who live among us without papers. The terms are clear:

We are a nation of laws. You broke the law. But we are also a nation of redemption. We are willing to offer you one chance—just one—to step forward, confess, and begin again.

Step one: Admit your culpability.

Step two: Pay restitution.

Step three: Stay in the United States.

Step four: Never become a citizen.

This is the deal. Dignity in exchange for accountability. Legal status in exchange for restitution. Step into the light, pay your dues, and in return, you will earn the right to work, to pay taxes, to travel freely, and to live without fear of deportation.

The genius of the plan is that it works for both sides. Republicans cannot call it amnesty—it requires real payment and real sacrifice. Democrats, who have long promised legal status, can finally deliver—but without a shortcut to citizenship.

It is not perfect. Nothing in Washington ever is. But it is fair. It is honest. And it is achievable.

The Dignity program is not simply about making undocumented immigrants pay. It is about using that money to make America whole again. Every dollar is accounted for, and every dollar is directed toward the public good.

Critics immediately objected. They said it was unfair to dock a dishwasher's pay by 1 percent when that worker already lives paycheck to paycheck. But they are missing the bigger picture. It is a small enough amount that Democrats can accept it, yet large enough in the aggregate to satisfy fiscal conservatives. It is not a burden—it is a bridge. A bridge to fairness. A bridge to order. A bridge to redemption.

This was always more than a policy choice. It was a principle. America is both a nation of laws and a nation of second chances. The Dignity Act was written to honor both.

THE COMPROMISE AT THE HEART OF DIGNITY

This is the compromise at the heart of the Dignity Act. Undocumented workers get to stay and work—but only if they pay restitution and accept accountability. American citizens reap the benefits of a fair labor system, stronger communities, and billions of dollars in new revenue.

Nobody gets everything. Nobody walks away untouched. Republicans cannot argue about border security—President Trump already delivered it. Democrats cannot demand citizenship—bringing people out of the shadows without amnesty is the only viable path. Business owners will adapt to it. Lives of the good immigrants will be changed for the better. And the American people will finally see a system that is both fair and enforceable.

Everyone sacrifices something for the greater good. That is what compromise really means. And for every lawmaker who supports Dignity, the reward is obvious: they walk away heroes. Heroes to the millions of Americans who demand order. Heroes to the millions of immigrants who crave stability. Heroes to a country desperate for a solution.

Win. Win. Win.

CHAPTER 5

How Dignity Benefits You—by Putting Money in Your Pocket

- Legalizing workers adds trillions to the US economy.
- The Dignity Act raises $70 billion to retrain American workers.
- The Dignity Act directly collects $50 billion to pay down the national debt.
- Dignity stabilizes food prices, housing, and supply chains by protecting essential labor.
- Dignity ensures our healthcare and caregiving sectors continue to deliver for aging Americans.
- New taxpayers secure Social Security and Medicare for future generations.
- More stability in labor markets means lower inflation and more opportunities for American workers.

THE MOST IMPORTANT ECONOMIC BILL IN CONGRESS

We know what happens without immigrants. Within a week, grocery shelves would be stripped bare. New homes would stop rising from the ground. Restaurants, tourism, and travel—cornerstones of American life—would become unaffordable for middle-class families.

This is not speculation. It is a fact. Millions of undocumented workers are powering these industries, and together, agriculture, construction, and hospitality account for roughly 15 percent of the nation's GDP. That's nearly one-sixth of our entire economy held together by people most politicians only talk about in whispers or soundbites.

Immigration isn't just immigration. Immigration is economics. Immigration is everything.

By now, we know what we stand to lose without immigrants.

If we fail to address and stabilize this dependency—comprehensively and thoughtfully—if we instead embrace the fantasy of mass deportation that hardliners love to promise, the consequences will crash down on all of us. Deport millions of workers overnight, and you won't just hurt immigrants. You'll ignite economic shocks that ripple through every sector: higher costs of living, runaway inflation, recession.

That's what we stand to lose without immigrants. Here is what we stand to gain—with Dignity.

The case is straightforward. The Dignity Act is not just good immigration policy. It is the single most important economic bill in Congress today.

With the growth unlocked by this legislation, we can actually begin to pay down our debt and restore fiscal responsibility—something Republicans have demanded for years but have been unable to achieve.

The mechanics are clear. The Dignity Act prevents long-term workers from being deported and allows them to fully and legally participate in the US workforce. That means filling urgent gaps in the labor market and capturing the economic benefits of their work through taxes, restitution fees, and growth of our critical industries.

It's not just about the present. It's the future. Through its legal reforms, the Dignity Act also prepares the United States for the next century: advanced manufacturing, artificial intelligence, financial technology, and cyber defense. These industries will define the next generation of global competition. Without workers—skilled and unskilled—we cannot lead them.

(By the way, we have not addressed legal immigration yet, but I will do that later in this book.)

Critics will keep shouting the same lines. "Immigrants are taking jobs. Immigrants lower wages. Deport them, and Americans will do better." Others argue we can just automate everything. Build machines to replace the workers. Or they suggest that deporting millions will magically solve the housing crisis. They say the economy will absorb the shock. They believe it won't affect them personally.

They are wrong.

The truth is that immigrants fill labor gaps—especially in sectors that native-born workers either cannot or will not fill. And they don't just work—they spend. They buy food, cars, and clothes. They rent homes, pay tuition, and open businesses. Every dollar they spend fuels demand for goods and services, creating more opportunity for Americans.

Immigrants grow the pie. They do not shrink it.

They complement American workers instead of replacing them, filling skill gaps that increase overall productivity. They create jobs rather than taking them. In fact, immigrant-owned businesses hire more employees per capita than businesses owned by the native-born.

That is not stealing from America. That is building America.

What's in it for you?

The answer is: a lot.

1. The Dignity Act Will Grow US GDP by TRILLIONS

Immigration is not just a social issue—it is the single biggest driver of our economic engine. Over the last two decades, immigration has been the primary source of growth in the American work-force. And as the baby boomers retire and the population ages, immigrants will be even more essential to keeping our labor force strong, our economy growing, and our nation globally competitive.

The Congressional Budget Office itself estimates that between 2024 and 2034 immigration will add **$8.9 trillion** to America's GDP. That's not wishful thinking—that's a sober, official projection.

And the Dignity Act supercharges this.

In fact, the Bipartisan Policy Center looked at the Dignity Act in its *Green Light to Growth* report. The analysis found that *just one aspect* of Dignity will produce over **$4 trillion** in GDP growth over just the next decade—an effective 14 percent expansion of our economy.

This is what happens when you unleash human potential.

2. The Dignity Act Raises $70 Billion to Retrain American Workers

This is not theory. This is the largest workforce investment in modern American history. Participants in the Dignity program will each pay $1,000 per year for seven years in restitution. Multiply that across millions of participants, and you have an unprecedented fund for American workers.

Every participant funds training for more than one American citizen. Apprenticeships. New skills. Higher education. Specialized instruction to prepare Americans for the jobs of the future—whether in construction, welding, HVAC, any number of other trades, education, public safety, advanced manufacturing, financial services, or AI.

For every immigrant who steps out of the shadows, an American gets a chance to step up into a better-paying career.

3. The Dignity Act Directly Collects $50+ Billion to Pay Down the National Debt

This is not just about growth. It's about responsibility. For decades, Washington has racked up debt without any serious plan to pay it down. As we speak, the national debt is $37 trillion and rising. (We spend more than we make.) The Dignity Act begins to reverse that trend.

Here's how: **1 percent Levy.**

Every worker under Dignity status pays a 1 percent income tax (levy) for seven years. The math is simple. In the first quarter of 2025, median weekly wages for US workers were $1,194, or about $62,088 per year. One percent of that is $620 annually—about $4,340 over seven years. Multiply that by millions of workers, and you can generate around $50 billion over seven years.

This provision creates a direct $50+ billion down payment on our national debt—the first serious bipartisan step in decades to actually start paying it back.

4. The Dignity Act Helps Save Social Security and Medicare

Economists have been sounding the alarm for years: workforce shortages are not just an inconvenience—they are an existential threat to Social Security and Medicare. If too few people are paying in, the programs collapse.

Once the workers come out of the shadows, the government can finally collect the billions in taxes currently left on the table. And here's the truth: the lazy caricature that undocumented immigrants don't pay taxes is simply false.

In 2022 alone, undocumented immigrants paid an estimated $96 billion in federal, state, and local taxes. That breaks down to roughly $15 billion in sales and excise taxes, $10 billion in property taxes, and $7 billion in personal income and business taxes. These are real dollars that keep the lights on in schools, pave local roads, and help fund hospitals.

And here's the kicker: undocumented immigrants actually contribute taxes at a higher rate than native-born Americans or even legal immigrant workers. They pay into systems like Social Security, Medicare, and unemployment insurance—programs they cannot access. They put in. They get nothing back.

The Brookings Institution recently released a study identifying the Dignity Act as a solution—not just to immigration, but to the solvency crisis facing these entitlement programs. Ensuring the millions of workers, who were previously working under the table, are now on the books and paying into Social Security and Medicare, stabilizes the system. At the same time, these workers never draw from those programs themselves. Net contributors. No drain. What a blessing.

This is not charity. This is survival for programs that millions of American seniors rely on to live.

And it is not only about numbers. It is about people. The same study found that the Dignity Act directly addresses critical workforce shortages in healthcare—nurses, home health aides, personal care assistants. These are the jobs that keep our parents and grandparents alive, and they are also the jobs we are running out of people to fill. Without them, the system collapses. With them, dignity extends to every American family.

5. The Dignity Act Solves the Labor Shortage and
Brings Market Certainty

As of June 2025, the United States had **7.4 million unfilled jobs.** Businesses across America are desperate. Farms, factories, hospitals, hotels. The Dignity Act is the only legislation in Congress that can solve the shortage overnight while also preparing for the workforce needs of tomorrow.

Critics will ask: Don't immigrants drive down wages? The short answer, backed by hard evidence, is no.

A major study from the National Bureau of Economic Research, *"Immigration's Effect on U.S. Wages and Employment Redux,"* found that immigration has a **positive and significant impact** on the wages of less-educated native workers—between +1.7 percent and +2.6 percent over the period 2000–2019. For college-educated workers, immigration had no significant impact. In other words, immigrants raised wages at the bottom and left wages unchanged at the top.

The study also found positive effects on employment for most native workers, even in the period from 2019 to 2022. No significant crowding out. No lost jobs.

The bottom line is clear. Immigrants don't take jobs. They make jobs. They raise wages. They strengthen markets.

That's what Dignity means—not just for immigrants, but for you.

Even so, nothing will help the American worker more than ending the informal economy, and its use of illegal immigrants, once and for all.

SAY GOODBYE TO THE BLACK MARKET— HELLO, E-VERIFY!

Deporting millions of workers would be a catastrophic mistake. But pretending the problem does not exist—ignoring the black market, shrugging off the lost revenue, looking the other way while illegal labor props up entire industries—is just as destructive. That's why the Dignity Act tackles both sides of the crisis head-on.

Right now, millions of individuals are working in America through an informal, largely unregulated shadow economy. It's not hidden in some alley—it's everywhere. In farms, hotels, restaurants, construction sites, and suburban homes. Americans are hiring these workers and paying them off the books, outside the formal legal and tax framework.

When companies want undocumented workers, they rarely hire them directly. They use middlemen. The business pays the contractor, the contractor pays the worker, and on paper, it all looks clean. But to make the books work, the worker needs a Social Security number. That number is easily bought—on the streets of Los Angeles, in the fields of West Texas, anywhere.

Suddenly, a young woman from Guatemala, Carla Gonzalez, becomes Rosa Perez, a dead woman in the United States. Her name, her social security number, stolen and sold. Taxes withheld, paperwork filed, the business gets cover, the worker gets survival, and the fraud rolls on.

Other times, the workers are paid in cash. No paperwork, no taxes, no protections. Wages are depressed for American citizens, because they may be paid under minimum wage. Communities lose revenue. And the national debt climbs higher.

This is not just an open secret. It is a fraud in plain sight. Every link in the chain is guilty to some degree. Workers. Employers. Middlemen. Everyone is complicit. Even the good people, the undocumented, who think they are just trying to get by, are, in reality, feeding a shadow economy.

Because this work is done in the shadows, the wages are suppressed. These men and women often receive less than what they'd earn if employed legally. That undercuts American work-ers, drives down wage standards, and distorts the marketplace.

The worst part? Businesses that want to play by the rules and only hire legal workers are punished. They get undercut by com-petitors who break the law.

Consider a hotel owner who dutifully checks every employee's eligibility. She plays by the rules, pays fair wages, and pays taxes. And what happens? She's punished—undercut by the competitor down the street who hires undocumented workers off the books for less. The cheater wins; the honest business loses. That is the system we've built. That is the rot we've allowed to spread. And that is what Dignity will end.

Closing these gaps is not just a matter of fairness—it is a matter of national economic security. Our ability to maintain American standards of living depends on tearing down this shadow econ-omy. Bringing it into the light raises wages, restores dignity to work, and forces every employer to compete on the same terms.

There is a tool to fix it: E-Verify. A federal system that allows employers to confirm work eligibility by checking a new hire's information against federal databases. It was launched in 1996, designed to be a safeguard. And yet, almost three decades later, it remains voluntary in most of the country. Yes, I said voluntary. The penalties for the business sector hiring illegal workers are laughable—barely a slap on the wrist. (The *real* question is: Why is it voluntary and not mandatory in the first place?! Don't even ask. It's the most hypocritical part of the whole system.)

The Dignity Act smashes this shadow system. For the first time in American history, it would make E-Verify mandatory nation-wide. Every employer. Every worker. Every time. No more patch-work of states—half enforcing, half not. No more wink-and-nod compliance. No more plausible deniability. President Reagan promised this in 1986, but Congress never delivered. Dignity fulfills that promise, nearly forty years later.

The penalties will be real, swift, and severe. And at the same time, the millions of undocumented immigrants who have already lived, worked, and contributed here will have the chance to come out of the shadows legally.

That is balance. That is justice. And it is how we protect both our economy and our values.

The real winner is the American worker. Wages for lower-wage earners will increase. They no longer have to compete against illegals working under the table or off the books. When we level-set and even the playing field, everyone wins.

We are giving undocumented workers a second chance. And we are giving business owners one chance—just one—to clean the slate, comply with the law, and move forward honestly. No penalties for the past. But total accountability for the future.

And that is exactly why business elites spend millions lobbying against it. They sit in congressional offices, they sit in the Oval Office, and they say: "If you make this mandatory, we collapse." And so, the same politicians who thunder on television about border security and accuse me of wanting to give amnesty to millions of Hispanics are the ones quietly protecting the very system that keeps it broken.

This is the hypocrisy at the heart of our immigration debate. Both parties know it. Both parties benefit from it. And both parties are guilty of letting it continue.

Enough.

No more lies. No more shadow games. A level playing field—for workers, for business owners, for every American.

A RISING TIDE LIFTS ALL BOATS

It's worth revisiting what happens if we fail to act.

The evidence on deportations is overwhelming. A University of Colorado study looked at the presidencies of George W. Bush and Barack Obama and found that for **every one million undocumented immigrants deported, 88,000 US native workers were driven out of employment.** Why? Because when you rip workers out of industries overnight, businesses don't magically find Americans to take the jobs. They cut back and stop investing in those industries. When the investment dries up, demand shrinks, and local economies spiral.

A Penn Wharton Budget Model study in 2025 reached the same conclusion, bluntly titled: *Mass Deportation of Unauthorized Immigrants: Fiscal and Economic Effects.* Its finding: "[I]t is well known that mass deportation reduces aggregate economic variables like GDP, the capital stock, and labor supply, simply due to scale effects." Deportations shrink not just the overall economy but also GDP per capita and average wages. In plain English: fewer workers, slower growth, smaller paychecks. Deportation hurts everybody.

History proves the point. Michael Clemens, writing for the Peterson Institute for International Economics, notes that when the Kennedy and Johnson administrations shut out most Mexican workers in the 1960s, it didn't create jobs for Americans—it created crises. Farmers scrambled to adjust, incomes dropped, land values collapsed. When Hoover and Roosevelt led the deportation of 400,000 Mexicans and Mexican Americans during the Great Depression, employment and earnings for US workers in the hardest-hit counties **fell**. Coolidge's crackdown in the 1920s? Same result: industrial production slashed, jobs destroyed.

Even Operation Wetback—Eisenhower's 1954 mass deportation campaign that the far right loves to glorify—didn't work without a parallel expansion of **legal pathways**. Eisenhower simultaneously expanded the Bracero Program, a bilateral agreement with Mexico allowing laborers to work legally and temporarily in America. The program, first born in World War II, kept our farms running while American men fought overseas and women entered the factories. Eisenhower understood the balance: if you take away workers, you must create legal replacements. He turned illegal workers into legal ones. That's the only reason the economy didn't collapse.

Immigration policy has always been about balance—about ensuring America has the workers it needs while protecting wages and standards of living. Deportation of long-term contributors upsets that balance. It shrinks industries, cuts investment, and destroys local economies. Giving them Dignity restores balance. It expands opportunity, raises wages, and grows the economy.

That is the fundamental choice before us. Keep pretending the black market is sustainable—or finally drag it into the open. Keep fantasizing about mass deportations—or accept reality and turn undocumented workers into documented, taxpaying, law-abiding residents.

The evidence is clear: if we legalize those already here, if we give them a pathway to Dignity, the entire economy grows stronger. Not just immigrants. Every American.

That is the promise of Dignity: not merely to avoid catastrophe, but to unlock the incredible, untapped potential of millions of people already living, working, and contributing here. The rising tide is waiting. All we have to do is let it lift every boat.

CHAPTER 6

Do You Know Who Your Neighbor Is?

- We have no idea who came in under President Biden.
- Dignity separates the contributors from the criminals.
- Dignity fixes our asylum system by creating humanitarian campuses to quickly process asylum seekers. It ends catch and release.
- Dignity turns invisible neighbors into accountable, contributing community members.
- Dignity allows ICE to home in on the real criminals and recent arrivals.

DIGNITY FREES ICE TO FOCUS ON THE BAD HOMBRES, AS PRESIDENT TRUMP CALLS THEM

When Donald Trump says the country has been invaded, he isn't wrong. Among them are the more than ten million people who came in under President Biden in the last four years: hundreds of individuals on terrorist watch lists. Thousands of criminals.

That leads to the most basic, urgent question: **Who the hell are these people?**

Until recently, the answer was at least predictable. Most migrants came from Mexico and Central America, drawn north by geography and opportunity. But everything changed once smugglers cracked open the Darién Gap.

We covered this briefly when discussing the caravans, but this is worth diving deeper into. For years, the Darién Gap—a wild, treacherous stretch of jungle between Panama and Colombia—was a natural barrier. Only a few thousand dared to cross each year, and most were young men from nearby countries. Families avoided it. The dangers were too high, the path too uncertain, the infrastructure nonexistent.

Then came 2021. Venezuela's economic collapse. Political chaos across the region. Biden elected president. People were desperate—and word began to spread: if you could make it to the southern border of the United States, you would be let in.

The coyotes—human smugglers—saw their opening. They mapped routes, cut trails, and set up checkpoints. They built an illicit business model on WhatsApp and Facebook, advertising the once-impassable jungle as a paid pathway to America. For a few hundred—or even a few thousand—dollars, you too could cross. And so the Darién Gap was reborn as a booming enterprise, and the flood was unstoppable.

And into that vacuum poured not only economic migrants and families fleeing hardship, but also bad actors—terrorists, traffickers, cartel operatives, people smuggling guns, drugs, and human beings. Maybe eight million people came to clean rooms and wash dishes. But two million others represented a threat.

Here's the truth: we don't know who they were then. And we don't know who they are now. What we do know is that terrorists and gang members, like Tren de Aragua and MS-13, systematically infiltrated America in the last four years. The scale of this infiltration is also unknown.

Until we take a full accounting of everyone inside our borders, we cannot guarantee the safety of the American people. We cannot separate those who came in search of dignity from those who came to do damage.

That means we must distinguish between the long-term immigrants—the good *hombres*—and the recent arrivals or the criminals hiding among them. But right now, the very tactics we're using—mass ICE raids, random arrests, the constant threat of deportation—make that separation harder, not easier. By driving millions further into the shadows, we blind ourselves to the truth. Immigrants won't report crimes, or go to the authorities to report dangerous people in their communities, like they used to do, for fear the law will turn on them.

Dignity changes that.

Just think about it. By bringing the long-term undocumented out of hiding, we gain the transparency to know who is who. ICE and Border Patrol can finally focus where they belong: on the traffickers, gang members, the cartel smugglers, the hardened criminals. Communities, no longer living in fear of indiscriminate raids, will begin to trust law enforcement again, and that cooperation will make it easier to catch the real threats.

This is the heart of reform: replacing chaos with clarity, replacing fear with trust, and freeing our agents to hunt predators instead of chasing dishwashers.

Only then can we answer the most important question: **Do you know who your neighbor is?**

THE ASYLUM GAME IS OVER

The second problem: how do we stop new criminals from coming in? How are we processing people—and what happens after we do?

Asylum and catch and release.

The Refugee Act of 1980 was meant to establish a standardized framework for processing those seeking asylum and to address the influx of refugees fleeing communism. It also gave the president the authority to set annual refugee admissions and prioritize groups, effectively laying the groundwork for the modern asylum system.

We are talking about the early 1980s. This was right around the time I was getting started as a journalist. I was still a general assignment reporter covering local news in Miami, fresh out of journalism school, when the wars in Central America—Nicaragua, El Salvador, Guatemala—began to heat up.

Watching from Miami wasn't good enough anymore. I wanted to see for myself what was going on. I wanted to get the stories firsthand, on the ground.

So I went to Central America—first to Honduras and later to El Salvador—to report on the conflicts. My first assignment took me to a war refugee camp in Honduras called Las Vegas. At the time, no one else wanted to go there. It was dangerous, and no other Western journalists had been able to go in and get footage yet.

Getting in was a harrowing experience I will never forget. In some places, the road itself forms the border between Honduras and Nicaragua—and we were driving on it. Just the week before, a *Newsweek* reporter had been traveling that same road when a landmine exploded beneath his car. The charred carcass of the vehicle was still there—a grim warning.

It was the first time I had faced death as a journalist. And when you come face-to-face with death, it's true what people say: your life really does begin to play like a movie before your eyes. Somehow, I made it through alive, my camera still rolling.

The footage from that trip earned me my first three Emmy Awards. It also set my course. I decided to stay in the field, to keep telling these stories from the front lines. Years later, I became the Central American Bureau Chief for Univision, stationed in El Salvador, giving me an even closer front-row seat to the conflicts in our backyard.

The dynamics in that area were complex, to say the least. On one side were President Reagan, the Salvadoran Army, the US-funded Contras in Nicaragua, and the political elite. On the other side: the FMLN guerrillas in El Salvador, the Sandinistas in Nicaragua, and the Soviet Union. It was regional, but it was also an extension of the same Cold War forces—communism, revolution, civil war—that had pushed my family out of Cuba three decades earlier. And just like in Cuba, it was the people who bore the worst of it—from both sides—suffering mass displacements, human rights abuses, and years of volatility.

These were violent, destabilizing conflicts, and they drove large-scale displacement. From 1981 to 1990, an estimated one million Salvadorans, Guatemalans, and Nicaraguans fled repression, many traveling through Mexico to the southern border to seek asylum.

Legally, asylum was meant to protect people fleeing direct threats of persecution or violence—criteria that clearly applied to those escaping Central America's civil wars. Yet, by 1984, only about 3 percent of asylum claims from Salvadorans and Guatemalans were approved. This was far lower than approval rates for asylum seekers from other regions, even though the Central American applicants often had strong evidence of direct threats to their lives.

The low approval rates became a moral and political issue. Critics argued that the asylum system was failing in its intended purpose. Eventually, the American Baptist Churches sued the federal government over its handling of these cases, and the lawsuit succeeded. The resulting settlement reshaped US asylum policy, ensuring that credible claims would be taken seriously and evaluated fully before being denied. Unintentionally, it also opened a door for economic migrants to enter the United States by claiming asylum, even if they did not actually qualify for it.

By the time Biden took office, claiming asylum had become one of the fastest and most common ways to enter the United States—and the immigration system's biggest flaw.

It didn't matter if you were from Uganda, Kazakhstan, Afghanistan, India, or China; if you showed up at the southern border and claimed asylum, you were allowed to enter and remain in the country while your case was processed—a practice known as "catch and release." Thousands upon thousands of Chinese, Tajiks, Indians, and Africans came in that way.

When someone shows up at the border claiming asylum, they're first screened for what's called "credible fear." This means the immigration officer must determine whether there's a significant possibility that the person could qualify for asylum—not necessarily that their story is true, but that it's plausible enough to warrant a hearing. The bar for credible fear is very low—basically, if there's even a 10 percent chance the person is telling the truth, they're allowed to move to the next step. (That standard has been raised a bit in recent years, but it's still relatively easy to clear.)

If they pass that initial screening, they're released into the country with what's called a Notice to Appear (NTA), an order to show up before an asylum judge, who will ultimately decide whether their claim is legitimate, and they can stay, or it's not, and they have to leave.

The problem is, the courts are so backlogged that the first available hearing might be seven years out. In theory, the asylum law is designed to protect people fleeing persecution, to give them safe harbor in our country. But in reality, once they're let in, they're often stuck in limbo for years. Many simply disappear into the country, never to be heard from again. In the meantime, some are creating a life for themselves in this country. Under this system, tracking asylum seekers and enforcing outcomes becomes enormously difficult.

This practice started back when far fewer people were coming through the border, and asylum cases could be handled quickly—sometimes within a week or two. Back then, asylum seekers would be held in designated facilities while their case was being processed.

As migration surged and detention facilities hit capacity—especially for families and children—the system buckled. Detention became unsustainable. Instead, migrants were released into the country to await judgment. Word spread quickly. People realized they could show up at the border, claim asylum—whether the claim was true or not—and vanish. They'd promise to return in seven years for their hearing. Maybe they would, maybe they wouldn't. Many did. Many did not. By then, families had been started, roots had been planted, and entire lives had been built in the United States.

Catch and release became a major point of frustration for Republicans—and not without reason. The process made it far too easy for individuals to disappear and nearly impossible for the government to track or manage them once they were inside the country.

Under Biden, nearly everyone who arrived at the southern border claimed political asylum. They would say things like, *"They're going to kill me in Honduras,"* or *"I'm being persecuted in China for my politics."* Historical data reveals that roughly 70 percent of asylum claims are ultimately denied. Judges review the cases, find them not credible, and order deportation. Yet with the years-long backlogs, by the time a decision comes down, the individual is often long gone, or may be your neighbor.

Republicans proposed various solutions in the last decade: holding asylum seekers in detention centers until their cases could be decided, or requiring them to wait in Mexico before crossing. Each option faced enormous pushback from the left, making them politically toxic and nearly impossible to pass through Congress. With lawmakers unwilling to find common ground—and with neither side wanting to touch immigration in any meaningful way—power shifted to the president. That is how President Trump was able to curb catch and release during his first term. That is how Biden brought it back in full force once he took office. With every new administration, enforcement shifted again. The border closed. The border opened.

This problem has been building for years. It existed under Obama. It even existed under President Trump. Under Biden, the sheer scale exploded. Republicans argue that the solution is simple: deny entry at the border or keep asylum seekers in detention until their cases are heard. Democrats, on the other hand, view those measures as inhumane and unacceptable.

At that time, Democrats were not offering a clear alternative. They avoided direct challenges to Biden's policies but refused to embrace the Republican proposals. The result was paralysis. The two sides were miles apart, locked in a standoff, and the system remained broken.

IT'S CALLED A HUMANITARIAN CAMPUS

People should not be released into the country until we determine whether they truly qualify for asylum. Plain and simple.

So the question becomes: where should they go, how should we process them, and how can we do it quickly?

The breakthrough of Dignity was to carve out a perfect middle ground. Instead of forcing people to wait in Mexico or locking them in detention for years, we proposed keeping them in federal custody—in newly created facilities which I have called **humanitarian campuses.** Under our framework, there would be no family separation. That was non-negotiable. Families stay together in the humanitarian campuses.

If someone applied for asylum under the provisions of the Dignity Act, they would be placed in one of these three campuses, which will be located along the southern border. Unlike a jail, the campuses would allow freedom of movement within the grounds. People would not be able to leave until their case was resolved, but they would be fed three meals a day, receive medical care and psychological support, have access to legal assistance and recreation.

Speed is the most important difference between this model and the current system. Our commitment is to resolve every asylum case within sixty days. If an individual cannot demonstrate a credible threat of persecution or violence, they are sent back home. Sorry. If the evidence is strong, asylum would be granted, and they would walk out the door legally recognized as residents of the United States. No loopholes. No gaming the system. No years of limbo. Just a fair, swift, and humane process.

To make this possible, much of the burden would shift away from overextended immigration judges and toward asylum officers—trained professionals capable of efficiently determining whether a case is legitimate. Officers would have sixty days to make a ruling. The most complex cases could still go before a judge, but the vast majority would be resolved quickly.

Humanitarian campuses, along with the additional asylum officers and support staff, would be funded by the 1 percent levy imposed on participants in the Dignity program.

This approach was crafted as a bipartisan solution. Democrats had grown deeply skeptical of border security under President Trump, especially after the wall debate. Yet as chaos escalated under President Biden, the politics began to change. The crisis at the border became impossible to ignore and threatened to explode into a political liability. Fortunately, there remain serious lawmakers—like my Democratic cosponsor, Veronica Escobar—who were willing to put politics aside and search for compromise.

Border security remains essential, but on its own, it is a half measure. A wall alone cannot stop the flow. A stronger, faster, more transparent asylum framework, like the one envisioned in Dignity, can close the loopholes, prevent abuse, and restore trust. It provides an orderly, humane system that protects those who truly need refuge while ensuring the law is respected.

DIGNITY AS A TOOL TO RESTORE ORDER AT THE BORDER—FOR GOOD

President Trump secured the border, but if we want that victory to endure, we have to codify it. His measures cannot live and die with one administration. Executive action is a Band-Aid; congressional law is surgery. Unless border security is enshrined in legal statute, the next president can undo it with the stroke of a pen. That is not order. That is Russian roulette.

No immigration proposal—no matter how well-designed, no matter how compassionate—can move forward without iron-clad border security. It is the immovable first condition. Every Republican knows it, every Democrat fears it, and every serious negotiator has to accept it. Republicans will never entertain allowing undocumented immigrants to stay unless the border is sealed. And truthfully, they are right. You cannot fix the system downstream if the flood upstream continues.

That is why, from the very beginning, when John Mark and I sat down to draft the Dignity Act, we looked backward before we moved forward. We studied precedent. In 2018, Republicans had attempted to pass a border enforcement bill—two versions, known simply as Goodlatte One and Goodlatte Two, named for Judiciary Committee chairman Bob Goodlatte. Neither passed, but both carried the endorsement of President Trump. And that gave us a head start.

John Mark combed through the legislative language. He lifted out the bones of what had already been drafted and refined, then restructured it so that Dignity could build on—not duplicate—the work that had already been done. To his credit, he understood something Washington too often forgets: there is no shame in using good ideas, even if they failed once. Failure is not always a verdict on substance; sometimes it's a verdict on timing.

This is how we built the Dignity Act. We took what we knew had bipartisan support, or what had already cleared one chamber of Congress, and we polished it. We didn't reinvent the wheel—we put better treads on it and mounted it on a stronger vehicle. Then we paired it with a new framework, one that neither party had ever been willing to fully test: if you are undocumented, you get to stay in the country but never have a path to citizenship, pay a fine, and live a dignified life in the promised land. By the same token—no more illegal immigration. Ever. Backed by a law, not empty promises.

All of it—every word—rests on one condition: border security.

Here is the reality. Until just recently, the United States had never made a full, onetime investment to actually secure the border. Decade after decade, the approach was piecemeal—annual appropriations, half measures, "emergency" funding bills that patched holes but never built the dam. The result was predictable: year after year, people kept coming. The border wasn't a policy failure; it was an operational one. And it was an operational failure because Washington never treated it like a national priority.

This year, that changed with the passage of HR 1—the *One Big Beautiful Bill Act*—in July 2025, which allocated nearly $150 billion for immigration enforcement and infrastructure. It is a historic investment, but there is a catch.

The funding came through budget reconciliation—a partisan maneuver. And reconciliation, by law, cannot carry major immigration policy changes if they don't affect the budget. So yes, the wall will be built as long as Trump is president, but the statutes governing asylum, detention, and enforcement remain unchanged.

In other words, we put money toward the border, but there is no law on the books to require the next administration to keep securing the border. And they can stop spending the money that was allocated in an instant. All they have to do is win the White House.

Which means the next administration could still reverse everything President Trump is doing, gutting the progress made. And make no mistake: someone will try. That is why codification matters. That means security policy for the southern border must be passed by Congress.

The fundamentals of border security have not changed in forty years. It comes down to three things: technology, infrastructure, and personnel. The border stretches nearly 2,000 miles. Only about 750 of those miles—across deserts, rivers, and rugged terrain—are lined with fencing or barriers. That leaves over 1,200 miles of wide-open opportunity. And when opportunity exists, smugglers, cartels, and coyotes will exploit it.

Technology has begun to change that equation. When we started drafting Dignity, Border Patrol was deploying infrared towers built by firms like Anduril and General Dynamics. Each tower covered about one mile, differentiating between animals and humans, all linked to a central command center. But by 2025, those towers had leapt forward. Now a single tower can monitor a five-mile radius. Hundreds are already in the field. One agent in one truck, guided by that technology, can control a ten-mile stretch of border. As soon as a migrant crosses, the system pings the exact coordinates, and agents intercept in real time.

Think about what that means. We were flying blind—agents on horseback, drones that only caught part of the picture, cameras that could be tricked. Now, we have the ability to see everything, everywhere, all at once. The technology exists. The only thing missing has been the political will and congressional directive to deploy it everywhere it is needed.

That is where Dignity comes in. Our bill requires, by law, that this gets done: more towers, more agents, more infrastructure, and mandatory technology upgrades. No more piecemeal. No more patchwork. No more endless debates about whether physical barriers work. They work. Towers work. Personnel works. The issue has never been capacity; it has been courage.

Courage is what Dignity demands. Because dignity starts with safety. Dignity starts with knowing who is entering your country and why. Dignity starts with the American people trusting that their laws mean something, and that those laws exist on the books to protect them.

That is what our proposal restores: not just order at the border, but faith in the system.

CHAPTER 7

The Largest Loss of Christianity in American History

- Mass deportations will devastate churches and trigger an unprecedented loss of Christianity in America. Fear is already affecting congregation attendance.
- The Dignity Act is rooted in biblical values: forgiveness, second chances, and restitution.
- Dignity protects the faith communities that keep families strong and society stable—while upholding the Judeo-Christian principles America was founded on.
- The religious community, of all denominations, is rallying around this solution.

A FAITH-BASED CASE FOR DIGNITY

It's no surprise pastors are calling me. They are scared. Among Latino congregations, 10, 20, sometimes 30 percent of their congregations are gone. Not vanished, not running from the faith—but hiding. Too afraid to show up at church. Too afraid to sing in the choir, sit in the pews, or send their children to Sunday school.

They are worried about ICE raids at church, worried about ICE picking them up *on the way* to church.

It's no wonder that Evangelicals, Catholics, Baptists, Methodists, Lutherans, and Pentecostals alike look at Dignity and are saying: *Finally, something to address this.*

We're a God-fearing country. America was built on Judeo-Christian values. We are a righteous, moral nation. I believe we need a solution—like Dignity—that reflects that.

The very name of the Dignity Act is not the product of a pollster or a consultant. It is from the Bible.

Genesis 1:27 teaches: "So God created mankind in His own image, in the image of God He created them; male and female He created them." From the very first chapter of Scripture, the lesson is clear: every human being is made in the image of God. And with that image comes dignity.

The Bible also teaches forgiveness and second chances. Colossians 3:12-13 says: "Put on then, as God's chosen ones, holy and beloved, compassionate hearts, kindness, humility, meekness, and patience, bearing with one another, and if one has a complaint against another, forgiving each other; as the Lord has forgiven you, so you also must forgive."

That is what the Dignity Act represents. Forgiveness. A second chance. We are not saying the undocumented did nothing wrong. They broke the law. But as Christians, we know grace is possible. As lawmakers, we can reset the law in a way that both honors justice and extends mercy.

The concept of restitution is central to this. Exodus 22:3 lays it down clearly: "Anyone who steals must certainly make restitution." Restitution is how the guilty make amends—by paying back what is owed, restoring their place in the community, and being made right under the law. That is what the Dignity Act requires. Those who crossed illegally must admit it, must pay restitution, and must contribute to the country.

Even the structure of the program—the seven-year duration—is rooted in biblical tradition. In Leviticus 25, Moses sets forth a seven-year debt cycle, culminating in release and restoration. The Dignity Act follows the same pattern. Seven years of accountability. Seven years of restitution. And then, restoration. The fines are paid, and you can continue living here and working.

Matthew 5:7 tells us: "Blessed are the merciful, for they will be shown mercy." Luke 19:8-9 shows us the model in action, when Zacchaeus, a tax collector who had cheated his neighbors, promised to repay them fourfold. Jesus declared, "Today salvation has come to this house." Justice and mercy hand in hand. Accountability and redemption together. That is the balance we are after. That is the balance the Dignity Act restores.

No immigration law in American history has been built so thoroughly on biblical values. And there is no better foundation.

The Bible itself is filled with the stories of immigrants, refugees, and exiles. Joseph, sold into slavery, was trafficked to Egypt. David, hunted by King Saul, sought asylum among the Philistines. Naomi fled famine, and her daughter-in-law Ruth found welcome in a new land—an economic migrant building a new life.

Daniel and his companions lived as exiles in Babylon, forced to serve a foreign king. Even the entire nation of Israel knew exile after the Temple was destroyed, forced to live in distant lands. When King Herod sought to kill the children of Bethlehem, Mary and Joseph fled with baby Jesus to Egypt. In this way, even Jesus himself was a refugee.

The Bible also gives us unambiguous instruction on how to treat foreigners. Leviticus 19:33–34: "When a foreigner resides among you in your land, do not mistreat them. The foreigner residing among you must be treated as your native-born. Love them as yourself, for you were foreigners in Egypt. I am the Lord your God."

The people of Israel knew what it was like to be strangers. And so do we. America is a nation of immigrants. Jesus reaffirmed this ethic when He said the greatest commandments are to love God—and to love your neighbor as yourself. He did not define who counts as "neighbor." He left no caveats, no exclusions.

Today, our greatest challenge is that our moral legacy is colliding with our laws. But laws can change. In fact, that is how democracy works. When our laws no longer reflect our values, our needs, or our national priorities, we have the power—and the responsibility—to bring them back into alignment.

That is the intent of Dignity. It is a policy that seeks to reflect both our values and the lessons of Scripture.

The stakes could not be higher.

If the Dignity Act fails, America risks the single largest forced loss of Christianity in our history. One in twelve Christians in the United States is undocumented or has a close family member who is. Indiscriminate raids and mass deportations, if continued, will rip entire congregations apart.

Imagine the pews emptying. Imagine the choir half gone. Imagine the fear echoing through the sanctuary. **America has never before adopted a policy that could so directly diminish the faith community.**

Not everyone is feeling it yet, because not all congregations are impacted equally. While some churches have few or no immigrants, others might lose half their members. It should matter to us all, though. The Apostle Paul describes the church as a body, made up of distinct but interdependent parts, and says that when one part of the body suffers, every part suffers with it.

That is why the Dignity Act has such strong support across churches. Pastors. Bishops. Evangelicals. Catholic leaders.

Denominations across the spectrum. Christians of differing theological traditions are banding together to raise the alarm.

They are calling their government leaders to ask them to intervene.

This is, truly, a reckoning of Biblical proportions.

All I can do now is pray to the Lord.

I hope you will join me.

CHAPTER 8

We've Been at This Crossroads Before

- America has faced immigration crises before; the pendulum has swung back and forth between extreme policies many times since the beginning of our republic.
- Every generation has benefited from the labor and energy of immigrants.
- When we have too much immigration, it leads to anti-immigrant sentiment.
- When we strike the right balance, immigration leads America to new heights.
- The question isn't whether immigrants will shape the future—it's whether we can strike the right balance and harness the potential of immigration to build the best possible future.

WHAT'S NEW IS OLD

America is the greatest country on earth, but our quest to become a "more perfect union" has never been easy.

One of the hardest, most persistent struggles has been over immigration policy: who gets to come, who gets to stay, and what it means to be an American. It's trying to find the right balance between security, the economy, and our values.

Make no mistake: the conversation we are having today is not new. Because we've been at this crossroads before. We can either choose between two extremes, or we can craft a solution that meets our needs at this time.

The pendulum has swung back and forth dozens of times across our history, and we can see the impacts.

If we are to truly understand what is at stake, we need to go all the way back to the very beginning.

One of Donald Trump's first actions upon returning to the White House in 2025 was to invoke the Alien Enemies Act—a law passed in the 1790s, in the earliest days of the Republic. That single fact should tell us something. **Immigration and national security were intertwined in America's politics before the ink on the Constitution was even dry.**

The debates and arguments around immigration are threads woven into the American story itself. From the beginning, the questions have been remarkably consistent: How do we safeguard national security and uphold the rule of law? How do we fuel economic growth? How do we meet our moral responsibilities as a nation that has long proclaimed liberty and justice for all?

Throughout history, we sometimes welcomed immigrants because it helped our economy, but other times because we believed it was the right thing to do. From settlers fleeing religious persecution in colonial times, to dissidents escaping totalitarian regimes during the Cold War, to families seeking safety from violence today—immigration has always been about balance.

Too much immigration, and you spark national backlash. Too little, the economy suffers, and we stray from our values.

1776: THE DECLARATION OF INDEPENDENCE

In the colonial era, many left Europe not only to escape hardship, but to claim rights they could never have under rigid European citizenship systems—rights like owning property, practicing faith freely, and securing futures for their children. The New World promised opportunity, and it delivered. The growing popularity of the American colonies started to worry England.

After the Seven Years' War with France, the Crown imposed restrictions on naturalization, limiting foreigners' ability to gain rights in the colonies. The restrictions were so severe that they made their way into the Declaration of Independence itself.

King George III was accused of "obstructing the laws for naturalization of foreigners, refusing to pass others to encourage their migration hither, and raising the conditions of new appropriations of lands." In plain terms: the colonists were saying, *We came here seeking opportunity, and now you are taking it away.*

We owe our independence, in large part, to immigrants. General George Washington's Continental Army relied heavily on Irish immigrants to fill its ranks. In fact, immigrants have played a key role in every major war in US history.

Surprisingly, the Constitution does not mention the word immigration. It did not spell out who could come, or under what conditions. But it did demand a uniform naturalization process. So Congress quickly passed the Naturalization Act of 1790—its second piece of major legislation. In other words, **the second most important piece of legislation that passed after we became a true nation was about immigration.** That shows you the importance of this topic.

It allowed citizenship after just two years—the shortest path in our history. (And Dignity has no path to citizenship—wow, things have changed.)

In 1795, Congress extended the naturalization period to five years and introduced the requirement of "good moral character," a concept that still echoes through immigration law today.

Soon after, the Alien and Sedition Acts were passed, including the Alien Enemies Act, which allowed us to arrest and deport members of a hostile nation. **Immigration was explicitly tied to questions of loyalty and national security.** The Alien Enemies Act would be invoked four times: against the British in the War of 1812; against Germans in World War I; against Germans, Italians, and Japanese in World War II; and in 2025 under President Trump, in response to waves of migrants that included cartel affiliates, gang members, and suspected terrorists. The Tren de Aragua gang, now a foreign terrorist organization (thanks to my efforts sounding the alarm about this in Congress), awoke the sleeping giant.

Already, within the first fifteen years after our nation was created, America had wrestled with immigration and security.

Now, we turn to our fledgling economy.

1800s: A YOUNG NATION

By the nineteenth century, attention shifted to who was arriving. Europe was on fire with famine, revolution, and unrest. Millions came to America. In 1840, the Irish Potato Famine drove waves of Irish immigrants to our shores. Germans came in large numbers as well, many skilled craftsmen. Congress and the public debated: were these immigrants taking jobs from Americans, or strengthening the economy?

Why do I believe this may sound familiar to you?

The Irish faced special hostility, not just because they were poor, but because they were Catholic. In a nation dominated by Protestant traditions, the arrival of millions of Catholics was viewed with concern, sparking fears over the religious and cultural impact of immigration.

We entered into the morality and values debate.

The year was 1848, when Europe convulsed with different rev-olutions—the "Springtime of Nations." Monarchs fell, republics rose, and thousands fled. Immigrants poured in from the collaps-ing Austro-Hungarian Empire. They came to America seeking not just bread, but freedom. We let them in, we prospered, and our economy grew.

Unfortunately, we were heading toward a civil war.

CIVIL WAR AND WESTWARD EXPANSION

The Civil War devastated our economy, and we had to rebuild what was lost. Abraham Lincoln, most famous for the Emancipation Proclamation, also recognized the value of immigrants. In a mes-sage to Congress near the end of that conflict, which lasted five years, he described immigrants as "one of the principal replen-ishing streams which are appointed by Providence to repair the ravages of internal war and its wastes of national strength and health." (So where are the GOP Lincolns of today?)

Because of Lincoln's influence, during the 1860s, two import-ant laws shaped immigration and settlement in the United States. The Homestead Act of 1862 offered up to 160 acres of public land to anyone willing to move west and develop land. In 1864, the Contract Labor Act encouraged immigration by allowing com-panies to pay for foreign workers' passage to the United States in exchange for a set period of labor. This policy helped businesses meet labor demands during rapid westward expansion, as we were rebuilding after the Civil War, and as we were entering the Industrial Revolution. Individuals did not have to be citizens to take advantage of these opportunities. There were very few limits on how many immigrants could come into the country through this program.

The pendulum had swung all the way open. It did not last long. In only two decades, the pendulum would swing back. In 1885, a new law prohibiting all contract labor was passed, in response to concerns about the increasing number of immigrants.

At the same time, the West Coast was popping. The California Gold Rush drew many Asian immigrants to that new, promising land. Chinese immigrants played a major role in building the country's infrastructure, particularly the Transcontinental Railroad, which connected the East and West coasts. Once again, concerns about jobs, culture, and religion ignited nativist movements, culminating in the Chinese Exclusion Act of 1882. Here we go again. The pendulum—back and forth. This remains the only law in US history that explicitly barred immigration based on a single nationality. (It was repealed in 1943, when China allied with the US against Japan during WWII.)

By now, it is crystal clear that these episodes illustrate a recurring pattern in American history. A group of immigrants arrives, contributes to the economy, and, within a few decades, faces backlash. Questions then arise about the "right" level of immigration in public debate. How many newcomers can be allowed or tolerated?

These historical cycles, from the beginning of the republic, have produced strong debate and argument. At such moments, we can either shut down completely or craft a policy tailored for that specific moment in time.

Let's see what happened as we entered the twentieth century.

By the early 1900s—roughly the midpoint between the Revolutionary War and today—there were intense debates about immigration. (What else is new?) Some reformers argued that immigrants obstructed the achievement of an ideal society, committed crimes, or abused welfare. (Fox News wasn't even on the air yet! But they sure would have been #1 in the ratings back then, as they are now.)

Scholars of the day advanced the idea that certain ethnicities possessed inherent qualities that would prevent assimilation into American society. These views contributed to restrictions targeting specific groups, including Jews, Asians, and Africans.

WORLD WAR I

During World War I, Congress passed the Immigration Act of 1917, which allowed for the detention and deportation of immigrants who committed certain offenses.

After the war, the United States faced the challenge of reintegrating more than four million returning soldiers into civilian life. With so many men needing jobs and the country adjusting to postwar conditions, Congress passed a series of laws to regulate immigration more strictly than ever before in the 130 years of our existence to that point.

The first law was the Emergency Quota Act of 1921, followed by the National Origins Act of 1924. These acts marked the first time Congress intervened so directly in setting limits and preferences for immigration. **Here is when we start truly deciding what nationality we prefer, and how many immigrants we are allowing.**

The Emergency Quota Act of 1921 established a cap of 350,000 immigrants from the Eastern Hemisphere. At the time, policymakers favored immigrants from Northern and Western Europe, such as England and France, considering them more "desirable." In contrast, Southern and Eastern Europeans, including Italians and Greeks, were viewed as lower-class or less assimilable. Under this system, 75 percent of the immigrants allowed under the quota were to come from Northern and Western Europe.

Before 1921, the game was inclusion. Everyone was welcome, except if you were on a blacklist. (To be fair, the list was long.) Why do I say that? US immigration laws largely focused on certain groups who were barred, but anyone not explicitly prohibited could immigrate. This 1921 act represented a major shift in our short history: the federal government now actively determined which immigrants could enter, how many could enter, and from what part of the world.

Within three years, Congress reinforced these restrictions with the National Origins Act of 1924, lowering the cap from 350,000 to 164,000. The act also shifted the regional percentages: more than 80 percent of immigrants would now come from Northern and Western Europe.

Where was the Western Hemisphere in this conversation? This is our backyard—from Mexico to Argentina. Ironically, the Western Hemisphere was not a concern at the time because there were so few people coming from Latin America or walking across the southern border. (Fox News would have lost all its ratings.) As the reader knows, this would change very quickly and dramatically.

It is in the 1920s that the now very familiar concept of "illegal immigration" emerges. Up to this point, for most of US history, there was no formal idea of illegal entry. Listen to this: people could arrive freely on our coasts, and unless specifically barred, they could eventually become citizens with no problem after waiting a period of time. More surprisingly, even if immigrants were barred from citizenship, many could still live in the United States without legal restriction. (Wow. What a world.)

Let me put it into context. At that time, there was very little government infrastructure and tracking, which made it relatively easy for immigrants to move within the country.

For example, someone arriving in New York could face challenges in the city, but could simply relocate westward to start a new life. The first generation of immigrants often remained culturally distinct, but their children—first-generation Americans, born in the United States—automatically became citizens and assimilated more fully, often loving and appreciating the country more than many of those who had been here much longer. I am a living, breathing example of this.

By 1932, the annual inflow of legal immigrants had collapsed to just 35,000. Think about that: in less than a decade, a country built on immigration had effectively cut off the flow of foreigners. This steep decline came only eight years after Congress imposed the quota system. It was one of the most dramatic turnarounds in American history. It was also a time of economic turmoil. For a nation that had once welcomed over a million newcomers each year, the gates were now nearly shut.

With fewer legal avenues available, many started coming into the country illegally. The federal government responded by inventing new ways to track, regulate, and punish those who snuck in. In 1933, the Immigration and Naturalization Service (INS) was created, the precursor to the Department of Homeland Security. For the first time, immigration was centralized in a federal agency designed not to welcome, but to control.

This is where our fight against illegal immigration began.

WORLD WAR II

As the 1930s gave way to the 1940s, suspicion hardened into law. Security was back at the forefront. In 1940, with the world once again at war, Congress passed the Alien Registration Act. Every non-citizen had to register with the federal government, provide fingerprints, and notify authorities of any change of address.

Communism was a threat. Therefore, political ideology also became grounds for deportation. Membership in a communist, fascist, or Nazi party was enough to get you expelled. America was now policing not just who entered, but what their beliefs were.

In 1942 came one of the most shameful episodes in our history: the internment of Japanese Americans. Following the attack on Pearl Harbor, more than 100,000 Japanese Americans were forced from their homes and placed in internment camps. Entire communities were uprooted. Families lost homes, farms, and businesses overnight. It was mass incarceration, justified by "national security," but in reality, it was fear—fear codified into policy.

The irony was painful. Up until this point, America had prided itself on being a refuge, even during difficult times. Jewish families fleeing pogroms in Eastern Europe had found safety here in the late nineteenth and early twentieth centuries. Political dissidents had sought shelter from czars and kaisers. Yet as Hitler rose in Germany in the 1930s, the United States closed its doors. Quotas limited immigration, and desperate families found nowhere to turn.

The most haunting symbol of this failure is the story of the *St. Louis*. In 1939, this ship carried over 900 Jewish men, women, and children fleeing Nazi terror. They then sailed to the United States, which refused them entry. The captain pleaded with American officials to let the passengers disembark. The refugees begged for sanctuary. But the FDR government turned them away. Forced to return to Europe, many of those passengers later perished in the Holocaust, in concentration camps run by the Nazis. The voyage of the *St. Louis* remains a stain on America's conscience—a reminder of what happens when immigration policy swings too far in one direction and is unable to adjust to the times. (The tragedy of the *St. Louis* is also a stain on Cuban history, as the ship tried to stop in Cuba and was turned away there as well. Cuban Americans owe a debt to the Jewish people.)

Even during World War II, the story of immigration was full of contradictions. With millions of American men overseas, labor shortages at home became acute, especially in agriculture and transportation. To fill the gap, in 1942 Washington created the Bracero Program, bringing Mexican laborers north under temporary contracts. These men harvested crops, maintained railroads, and kept the economy moving.

Shortly after, in 1954, the government launched Operation Wetback, an effort to deport Mexican workers who were here illegally. On one hand, we invited laborers in. On the other, we expelled them. The contradiction revealed the fundamental tension that runs through our immigration story: America depends on immigrant labor, yet fears it at the same time.

How do we balance this? (In psychological terms, it's called neurosis. You want the object and its opposite at the same time.)

The pendulum is about to swing back again. Just watch. In 1952, Congress stepped in to again to address the reality of the labor force needs with the Immigration and Nationality Act. The act expanded quotas, repealed old restrictions on contract labor, and created formal categories for guest workers. Most significantly, it introduced family petitions as a cornerstone of US immigration policy. This law laid the groundwork for the legal immigration system that still exists today.

America was about to boom.

By now, this is an old movie. How many more times do we need to watch it?

THE COLD WAR

Then came the Cold War, and immigration took on a new role—as a weapon of ideology. Welcoming refugees from communist regimes was not just charity; it was strategy. Every Cuban who fled Castro, every Hungarian who escaped after the 1956 uprising, every Vietnamese family airlifted during the fall of Saigon—they all became living proof of America's superiority over the Soviet Union. **Immigration promoting American values was back.**

In 1965, Congress doubled down on this new immigration policy and passed the Immigration and Nationality Act of 1965. Signed by Lyndon Johnson at the foot of the Statue of Liberty, the law abolished the national-origin quotas that had favored Northern and Western Europeans. In their place came a new preference system: 75 percent of green cards would go to family members, about 20 percent to employment-based immigrants, and roughly 5 percent to refugees. Spouses and parents received the highest priority. More distant relatives—adult children, siblings—entered long lines. This is where the so-called chain migration started. You came because you knew somebody, not because of what skills you had. Employment visas, limited in number, became the secondary pathway. Refugees were accepted, but in relatively small numbers.

The 1965 law opened America's doors wider than they had been in decades. It also created new challenges. By emphasizing family ties, it did less to accommodate the country's actual labor needs. Many lower-skilled workers came legally through temporary visas but stayed after their permits expired. Others crossed without authorization.

America continued to prosper, but we could not figure out how to control illegal immigration. Over time, the undocumented population grew, creating a new imbalance.

This is the situation that President Reagan inherited in the 1980s. We already know what happened afterward.

TODAY, TOMORROW, AND INTO THE FUTURE

History teaches us this: American immigration policy swings like a pendulum. We open, then we close. We welcome, then we fear.

We deport, then we legalize. This is exactly where we are now under President Trump.

The faces of the migrants may change—Irish, German, Italian, Greeks, Chinese, Jews, Mexican, Salvadorans, Cubans, Dominicans, Venezuelans—but their motives do not. Economy, security, morality, and the pull of the American dream. Always the same themes, framed in new ways.

What is different today is not the debate itself, but the failure of Congress to meet the moment. In recent decades, lawmakers surrendered immigration authority to the executive branch. Presidents of both parties have governed by executive order. Congress is absent.

Obama swung the pendulum open with DACA. President Trump closed it with Title 42. Biden swung it open again with the migrant caravans. President Trump sealed the border and is ramping up mass deportations. But in 2028, a new president can rescind all the money allocated to secure the border. And the movie starts again. And it could be even scarier.

I don't believe this is the appropriate way to handle a crisis that affects every American community. Until Congress steps up to do its job, with a durable, bipartisan framework enshrined in law, immigration policy will remain at the mercy of whoever sits in the Oval Office. And the chaos in our immigration system will remain with us.

How will history look back on this time? I don't know.

What I know is this: I am in Congress, and I am doing my civic duty by writing this law. A law that meets this moment, instead of embracing one of the extremes. While others run around in fear, I feel like Caleb from the Bible—the scout who saw the opportunity the Lord had promised, even though the mission ahead would not be easy. When everyone else was terrified of giants in the Promised Land, and did not want to move forward, Caleb stood firm and said, "Yes, we can take it."

We're at a crossroads. We need a solution that meets the moment. We need to reclaim the Promised Land.

CHAPTER 9

"Why Don't People Just Come In the Right Way?"

- America is on the verge of a new era of growth—if we make smart choices now.
- While we stop illegal immigration, we should modernize our legal immigration system, which is also broken.
- Immigration, dignified and legalized, is the fuel for the next Golden Age.
- Harnessing labor, entrepreneurship, and innovation strengthens American and our global leadership.
- Failure means decline, shortages, and the loss of America's edge in the world.

BECAUSE LEGAL IMMIGRATION IS EQUALLY SCREWED UP

As we've covered, illegal immigration is the most pressing political issue of the day. What about legal immigration, though? One of the most common pieces of feedback I receive is people, understandably, asking: "Why don't people just immigrate the right way?"

The answer may come as a surprise: the "right way" just does not exist. Legal immigration is not what many people think. There is no single "line" to just wait in. This system is broken at every step.

Ironically, it's easier to come into the country illegally than to do it the right way. Immigrants can come to the US legally in only three ways—through a job, through family sponsorship, or through humanitarian protections like asylum—and every route (except asylum) is capped and heavily restricted.

In short, it has become extremely difficult to legally come and work in the United States. As the American Immigration Council points out: "[A]n immigrant from Mexico may be forced to wait anywhere between five and 25 years to become a naturalized U.S. citizen. If they're an immediate relative of a U.S. citizen—like a spouse, parent, or minor child, the total timeline is usually about five to seven years. This includes the wait for a green card, the residency requirement, and naturalization process. By contrast, most family-based immigration from Mexico involves much longer wait times. Spouses and minor children of legal permanent residents often wait two to four years for their own green card, resulting in a total of eight to 10 years before naturalization. Adult children and siblings of U.S. citizens face the longest delays, with visa backlogs that can exceed 20 years."

There are too few permanent work visas. The system for obtaining them is outdated, restrictive, and painfully slow. We need to reform the work visa system so employers can legally hire the workers they need—out in the open, above board, and ensuring they are not taking a job away from an American.

Remember, this reform—the legal migration, I mean—will take place as we are stopping illegal immigration once and for all. No more illegals, no more shadow economy.

As I just explained, the majority of the current US legal immigration system is family-based, meaning immigration is primarily determined by **who** you know in the country, not **what** you know. Therefore, the only real "right way" to come here is to already have a family member here.

Only about 15 percent of the annual permanent immigrant visas we issue—the so-called green cards—are set aside for workers who meet our economic needs. That leaves the vast majority of legal visas tied to family reunification, not to labor or talent. Right now, the United States provides just 140,000 employment-based (EB) legal work visas per year. That number was set in the early 1990s—before the internet, smartphones, AI, Silicon Valley, Amazon, Apple, Google. The world exploded, while our immigration system is still in the Stone Age.

Compare the 140,000 work visas to today's civilian labor force of approximately 170 million American workers, and you can see just how far apart these numbers are. Getting one of these visas is extremely difficult—and very competitive.

To those who believe foreigners are taking jobs from Americans, 140,000 is .0008 percent—a fraction of a fraction of a percent of our labor force.

Those 140,000 positions are divided into five categories, from EB-1 through EB-5. Each is supposed to address a different kind of worker. In theory, it's a rational design: match talent to opportunity. In practice, it is a maze of backlogs, bottlenecks, and bureaucratic delays. And not enough for what the free market needs.

Let's review the categories:

1. EB-1 is reserved for the best of the best; those with
   extraordinary ability. For instance, leading researchers,
   top executives, Nobel prize winners, and Emmy award
   winners. Albert Einstein and Taylor Swift (if she were not
   born in America) would have qualified for this visa, but
   it's extremely difficult to obtain. Because of that, it is the
   only category that does not have a major backlog.

2. EB-2 is for professionals with advanced degrees, like
   master's or doctorates. A cancer researcher from Japan, a
   successful businessman from Chile, or Dr. Yu, a surgeon
   who performs cataract surgery, would qualify. There is
   always a very long wait, specifically for people who come
   from populous countries like Mexico, India, China, and
   the Philippines.

3. EB-3 covers skilled workers, professionals without
   advanced degrees, and some unskilled laborers. This is the
   catch-all category, and many professionals fall under it.
   For example, it could be a skilled mechanic from Bolivia,
   a pharmacy technician from India, or a construction
   worker from Spain who practices a very specific form of
   masonry. As broad as it is, it is equally slow because it's
   very oversubscribed. It is one of the slowest categories to
   move through.

4. EB-4 is set aside for special groups, such as religious
   workers or individuals who have assisted the US
   government abroad. Thanks to this category, a priest
   from Ireland can come hold mass over a congregation in
   Boston. And a translator from Afghanistan who saved
   American lives on the battlefield can come and live in
   America.

5. EB-5 is for the rich immigrants—the foreign investors
   bringing capital to open businesses and create American

jobs. Incredibly, this category is also backlogged. I thought that money talks . . . but not when it comes to immigration. The richest man in the world must still wait in line.

It is not just the number of visas that creates the backlog—geography also plays a role. We may all be equal in the eyes of the Lord, but not every country is equal in the eyes of US immigration law. Treatment varies widely depending on where an immigrant is coming from.

Decades ago, Congress imposed a rule: no more than 7 percent of green cards, in any given year, can go to immigrants coming from one specific country. The idea was to preserve diversity; but in practice, it has created enormous backlogs for countries with large populations like India, China, Mexico, and the Philippines.

Consider this absurdity: if an American company wants to sponsor and legally hire a highly qualified employee from Mexico, it could take years—sometimes decades—before that person receives a green card, simply because the quota for that country has already been met.

Lo siento, Pepe.

Even when an employer is willing to navigate the bureaucracy, they may wait years to get the worker they need. A technology company could wait for years to fill a position they need today, which is not how any functioning economy works. That is a flashing red warning light: the system is broken.

The Dignity Act includes provisions to make the system more effective and more responsive to real-world needs.

The first idea is doubling the country cap—raising it from 7 percent to 15 percent. That will allow for the marketplace to bring in talent from more populous countries, if we deem it necessary.

That single adjustment would dramatically reduce backlogs for the largest countries, while still preserving the ability to bring in talent from around the globe. In a world where skills and industries change rapidly, we should not be arbitrarily tying one hand behind our back, limiting where we can draw talent from.

Another fix in the Dignity Act deals with what the experts call the "derivatives," a mathematical term used by bureaucrats. Remember how I explained that we only give 140,000 visas for employment each year? It happens that many of those workers applying have families—a spouse and children. According to government math, each child counts as if they were mathematicians or engineers coming into the country. Even if they have twelve children. And the stay-at-home wife counts too. This is ridiculous.

In practice, this means that only 30 percent of those 140,000 slots we just discussed go to workers themselves. Isn't this crazy? Only one-third of what is promised is delivered.

The Dignity Act solution to this is straightforward: exclude "derivatives" from the 140,000 cap. Count only the breadwinner, not their spouse or kids. Families could still come, but if they are not part of the labor force, they would not take away a slot meant for a hired hand. This change would not raise the overall immigration quota numbers, but it would guarantee that all labor slots go to actual workers. This would reduce backlogs significantly. We are giving so few work visas anyway, we might as well make each one of them count.

These two provisions in the Dignity Act, simple as they are, will streamline the system to make it more effective and responsive to our labor market needs, updating our system for the twenty-first century.

It is how you unlock our potential to create a workforce capable of winning the race in artificial intelligence, beating China, continuing to be the number one military in the world, and bringing back manufacturing to the United States.

If we want to bring America to new economic heights—and stay there for decades—getting legal immigration policy right is as important as securing the southern border.

As I've said repeatedly, immigration is not just about the border. It is about the future and America's place in the world.

I just mentioned manufacturing.

One of President Trump's stated goals is to bring manufacturing back to the United States. Yet today, there are roughly 420,000 manufacturing jobs sitting unfilled.

At the same time, sustained economic growth of 3 percent or more is critical if we are going to keep the United States competitive and ensure the standard of living most Americans expect. The truth is, we cannot consistently reach and sustain 3 percent economic growth if we cannot fill critical jobs, both today and fifty years from now.

How are we going to spark a true manufacturing renaissance without immigrants and without legal immigration reform? If we want to fortify America's industrial strength, we cannot do that without the Dignity Act.

If we cannot bring in the brightest minds and the strongest workers from around the globe, we will fall behind. The future of power is not only measured in tanks or missiles; it is measured in patents, in labs, in code, and in new ideas. It is measured in who wins the race for artificial intelligence, cyber dominance, and advanced manufacturing.

Right now, China is outproducing us five to one in PhDs. The Chinese Communist Party (CCP) has built an entire state-sponsored pipeline to identify, cultivate, and retain STEM experts. They are educating a new generation of engineers, mathematicians, and scientists. They are also recruiting talent abroad through programs like the "Thousand Talents Program," dangling lucrative offers to lure researchers—including many educated here in the United States—to return home and work for Beijing's interests. And they are succeeding.

The CCP is working aggressively to increase return rates for Chinese-born students who study overseas. China is already the top country of origin for international students in the United States, particularly in advanced STEM fields. Too many of them graduate from our universities with cutting-edge skills only to be forced out because our immigration laws cannot accommodate them. We are educating the world's best—and then kicking them out. It is insanity.

In 2022, fifty former national security officials from both Republican and Democratic administrations sounded the alarm in a public letter. Their message was blunt: "China is the most significant technological and geopolitical competitor our country has faced in recent times. With the world's best STEM talent on [the US] side, it will be very hard for America to lose. Without it, it will be very hard for America to win." They were not exaggerating.

Here at home, only half of the PhDs awarded by American universities go to US-born students. The other half are foreign-born. Many of them want to stay here, start families, and contribute to our economy—but they cannot, because our legal immigration system is restrictive, outdated, and broken, and does not accommodate this.

If we are serious about winning the battles that will define this century—cyber warfare, AI supremacy, breakthroughs in biotech and medicine—we must align our immigration laws with our national interests, as we have done in the past. We must make it possible for top global talent to stay in the United States, not push them out. This has always been a competitive advantage of ours.

The Dignity Act delivers that fix. It ensures that individuals *already here* pursuing PhDs in STEM fields will qualify for the O-Visa—reserved for people of extraordinary ability—allowing them to remain here for a time and work after graduation. It extends the same opportunity to medical doctors, addressing the physician shortage that is already straining hospitals and rural clinics across America. It is simple, it is fair, and it is vital to our national security. If they want to be an American, this gives them time to stay and compete for one of the 140,000 annual green cards we provide for talented workers.

America has always led the world because it attracted the best. We welcomed Albert Einstein and the German scientists who helped us win World War II. We brought chemists, medical researchers, and engineers from Asia and Europe. We created an ecosystem where the most brilliant minds wanted to be. Google cofounder Sergey Brin came here as a child refugee from the Soviet Union. Elon Musk chose the United States as the place to launch SpaceX and Tesla. How many Einsteins are we turning away today? How many Musks are now building their futures in other countries—some of them adversaries? What is the cost of our inaction?

Immigrants not only bring genius; they bring entrepreneurship. Forty-five percent of the Fortune 500 companies were founded by an immigrant or their children. 3.2 million immigrants currently run their own businesses, representing one out of every five entrepreneurs in the United States. Those businesses employ eight million American workers and generate $1.3 trillion in annual sales. That is not charity. That is fuel for our economy.

The data is overwhelming. According to the American Action Forum, for every 100 high-skilled immigrants, 183 jobs are created for native-born Americans. For every 100 low-skilled immigrants, 464 jobs are created for the native-born. Well-regulated immigration is not a zero-sum game. It is a force multiplier. It expands the economy, creates demand, and builds wealth.

Immigration also drives productivity. It introduces new skills and allows American workers to specialize, raising wages across the board. For every 1 percent increase in immigrant employment in a state, incomes rise by half a percent. Immigrants are disproportionately entrepreneurial. They take risks, they innovate, and they expand opportunity for everyone.

So ask yourself: if we shut that tap off—and on the legal side, we essentially already have—what does the future of America look like? Fewer jobs. Slower growth. Less innovation. Higher dependence on foreign supply chains. More power ceded to Beijing.

Some on the right still cling to the false belief that there is a finite number of jobs, and that every immigrant "takes" one from an American. It is nonsense. Immigrants create jobs—through investment, through entrepreneurship, through building businesses. There is no hard cap on the American Dream. We can all achieve it together. We have never reached our limit on job creation, and if we have a healthy economy, we never will.

The stakes are real. China is rising. The technologies of tomorrow are emerging at lightning speed. The global economy is shifting. And the question is simple: do we want to lead, or do we want to fall behind?

The status quo will not get us there. Only by embracing both the workers already here and the top talent of the future can America win. Only with Dignity do we secure our spot as the economic leader of the free world for generations to come.

CHAPTER 10

Amnesty Is *Always* the Boogeyman

- There are forces at work designed to fearmonger and distort the truth anytime someone wants to have a serious conversation about immigration reform.
- Every reform debate gets shut down by fearmongering about "amnesty."
- Dignity is not amnesty—no path to citizenship, no free pass, no shortcuts.
- Instead, it demands restitution, work, and accountability from every participant.
- Getting immigration reform through Congress carries political risk, and will require enormous courage.

FEAR

Why is it so hard to get immigration reform through Congress?

Of all the controversial issues we wrestle with in Washington—and there are many—why is immigration the single hardest one?

One word: **fear.**

When I first came to Congress, one of the first things I did was start walking the House floor, talking to other members. Democrat, Republican—it didn't matter. I didn't know anyone, and nobody really knew me. I came from outside the world of politics.

So every day, John Mark would hand me a list of five members to speak with. Next to each name was a short file: where they stood on immigration, a little about their district, and anything I could use to break the ice.

Then I'd head to the House floor—the great chamber where Members of Congress gather to vote. Picture it: a sea of dark suits, red and blue ties, the buzz of conversation, and that invisible but unmistakable division down the middle of the floor. Democrats on one side, Republicans on the other. You can literally feel the energy shift when you cross from one side to the next. It isn't just symbolic—it's tribal.

I'd spot a member from my list, walk right up, and introduce myself.

"Hi, I'm Maria from Miami. I want to talk to you about immigration."

Now they call me "Social Salazar" because I'll talk to anyone, anywhere. But back then, I was just a freshman Congresswoman with a mission, not to mention a minority woman with a Sofia Vergara accent, who spoke loudly and waved her arms around to drive home a point.

We'd sit down right there on the floor while votes were being called, so sometimes I'd stop to cast my vote, then pick up the conversation where we left off. I'd give them my pitch: it's time to fix immigration. It's the right thing to do. I'm working on a proposal called the **Dignity Act.** I'd explain the basics, answer a question or two, and then move on to the next. Sometimes I had to pause mid-conversation to cast my vote, then circle back to finish the pitch. It was like speed dating, but without hugs and kisses involved. Just policy.

These conversations couldn't happen in the halls. Too risky. Staffers everywhere, reporters circling like sharks, looking for a stray comment. On the House floor, though, it's member-to-member. No cameras. No soundbites. You can be candid, even blunt.

Outside, John Mark would be waiting.

"How many did you talk to?" he'd ask.

I'd tell them who listened, who shrugged me off, and who said "maybe."

At first, it was about sheer volume—talking to as many members as possible, testing the waters, and trying to figure out just how toxic this issue really was.

With Republicans, I had a go-to opener: "How do people in your district feel about immigration?"

The answers varied. Some were thoughtful. Others vague. Most tried to change the subject.

So I'd press them.

"What's the Hispanic percentage in your district?"

They'd give me a number: 13 percent. Fifteen percent. Twenty-two percent. That's if they knew. Most didn't have a clue how many Hispanics they had in their districts.

"Have you talked to that 22 percent? Do you know what they think?"

That's when the hedging started. "Yeah, yeah, of course. But…"

"But what?" I'd push. "Don't you think their voices matter? Don't you think they have important views on immigration? Why not join me?"

They'd listen politely, nodding, but I could see it in their eyes—they just weren't hearing me. Maybe they thought I was naïve. Maybe they thought I was crazy. But I didn't care. I was on a mission, and I had the receipts. John Mark, my partner in writing and strategy, had pulled every member's voting record on immigration. So I had ammo.

"You voted for this in 2013," I'd remind them. "Do you still stand by that? Do you still believe it?"

Some were caught off guard. Others respected the fact that I'd done my homework. Either way, they were learning: I was serious.

Here's what I discovered, almost immediately: very few wanted to touch the issue. Most would just throw up their hands. Republicans said, "Not until the border is secure." Democrats said, "Not unless there's a path to citizenship." Each side pointing at the other, waiting for the impossible.

But through those conversations, the truth crystallized. The real reason immigration reform has been impossible for so long is that Congress is paralyzed by fear. Point blank.

Most lawmakers are risk-averse. Their top priority isn't solving problems; it's survival. Getting reelected. Keeping the seat. And if staying in office is your only goal, then the last thing you want is to step into an issue that will get you attacked from both the left and the right. Immigration is exactly that kind of issue. For most, it simply isn't worth the risk.

I'll never forget one conversation with a colleague from the Midwest—a genuinely good man, decent, sincere.

"I want your support on immigration," I told him.

"And I want to support you," he said. "We need immigration. My district's full of dairy farms. We need the labor. We can't survive without it."

I jumped on it. "We've been working with the dairy associations. We've talked to the farmers. They love the bill."

He looked me in the eye. "But immigration?" He hesitated. "I just don't know if I can do it."

"Why not?" I asked. "You just told me you need it."

He leaned in close, lowering his voice so no one else could hear. "I don't know if I have the balls," he admitted.

Crude? Maybe. But it was honest. Brutally honest. (He's a nice guy, too, and a friend.)

Unfortunately, he wasn't alone. Over and over again, I heard the same thing—sometimes dressed up in careful political language, sometimes whispered in plain words: *I'm afraid*. Afraid of the headlines. Afraid of the attack ads. Afraid of the White House. Afraid of what the president is going to think. Afraid of being branded with one word that kills every immigration debate before it even starts: **amnesty.**

That fear is the shadow that hangs over every conversation in Congress about immigration.

THE MOST TOXIC WORD

Amnesty—perhaps the most toxic term in the most toxic issue in all of American politics. Amnesty is the boogeyman of immigration reform. It is the scarlet letter, the word that ends debates before they even begin.

Amnesty can mean many things to many people. But generally speaking, it means the willingness to give a free pass to those who snuck in and have lived illegally in this country. (The good news is Dignity is not amnesty—I am not making it easy on the illegals at all. They have to earn their status.)

Seizing on this weaponized word, the moment a Republican even considers a conversation on legalizing the undocumented, the vocal anti-immigration groups—FAIR, NumbersUSA, and others—come after them. They accuse them of supporting amnesty, by which they try to scare people into thinking they support a free pass to break our laws and get away with it.

These groups are not fly-by-night organizations. They are institutions decades in the making.

The Federation for American Immigration Reform (FAIR) was founded in 1979 by John Tanton, a man described by one of Ronald Reagan's aides as "the most influential unknown man in America." Tanton had an unusual trajectory. He began his career on the left, with groups like the Sierra Club and Planned Parenthood. But over time, his focus shifted almost obsessively toward anti-immigration policy, and he shaped national discourse by lobbying for restrictive legislation, publishing position papers opposing immigration, and providing testimony at congressional hearings.

In 1996, one of Tanton's protégés, Roy Beck, founded NumbersUSA. Unlike FAIR's think-tank model, NumbersUSA was designed to mobilize the grassroots. They built enormous online networks, used sophisticated call and fax campaigns, and created a system to overwhelm congressional offices with noise. While FAIR worked on the inside, NumbersUSA built pressure from the outside.

Together, these groups—and Tanton's other creations, like the Center for Immigration Studies (CIS)—reshaped the national conversation. They were instrumental in derailing President George W. Bush's 2007 Comprehensive Immigration Reform Act, a bill that had bipartisan support and a real chance of passage. To many, it looked like a serious compromise at the time. But FAIR and NumbersUSA went to work.

NumbersUSA sent more than a million faxes to senators, jamming their machines. FAIR mobilized conservative talk radio hosts, who denounced the bill as "amnesty" night after night. Congressional phone lines melted down under the volume of calls. A Republican staffer at the time admitted: "The fax machines would run out of paper. They have a hold, an influence. Most of what they do is try and scare members." It worked. The bill collapsed under the weight of that fear. Eighteen years ago.

Now, to be clear: these groups have a right to advocate for their vision of America. They believe immigration should be tightly restricted, and some Americans agree with them. That is a legitimate position. The problem is not their existence—it is their tactics. They are disingenuous in the way they operate. They don't want a debate. They don't want to weigh trade-offs or examine all the data. They want to weaponize fear. They turn "amnesty" into a dirty word that scares lawmakers into silence, even though no one knows what it means.

Imagine if we could actually have a national conversation about immigration levels. Should we admit one million people a year? One and a half million? Five hundred thousand? What skills should we prioritize? Who should come first—workers, family members, refugees? Should we go into a merit-based system like Canada and Australia? Should we allow the marketplace to dictate how many workers we need?

These are real policy questions. They deserve serious answers. FAIR claims to want to talk capacity. NumbersUSA claims to want to talk numbers. But instead of opening the debate, they slam it shut with accusations and scare tactics.

No wonder a politician has to be exceedingly careful with the word "amnesty." Even if you never use it, they might accuse you of supporting it anyway. The truth is, there is no agreed-upon definition of amnesty. But politically? It's poison. It's the word that will be hurled at any Republican who dares to touch immigration reform.

It's become a game of Whac-A-Mole. Any Republican who pops their head up and says, "Maybe we should fix this system"—whack. The attacks come instantly. Robocalls hit their district: *"Did you know Congressman X supports amnesty? He wants illegals flooding into our neighborhoods. He wants to hand out citizenship like candy."* Mailers show up in mailboxes. Talk radio lights up. It doesn't matter if the proposal has enforcement, account-ability, restitution, paying a fine, no path to citizenship ever. The word "amnesty" obliterates nuance.

The irony is that true amnesty—defined as blanket forgiveness with no consequences—rarely exists in modern immigration pol-icy within the Republican party. Many Democrats, on the other hand, have effectively embraced what amounts to what I believe is true amnesty—though they, too, avoid using the word.

In January 2021, on his very first day in office, President Joe Biden unveiled the US Citizenship Act. It was a sweeping, one-sided proposal. There was no serious border security component, just a promise to "study" the issue, which in Congress-speak means: do nothing. For the undocumented already here? Congratulations, you're now a citizen with no strings attached. And it did nothing to stop illegal immigration.

For Republicans, it was the nightmare scenario: a mass legal-ization with no plan to secure the southern border, which would guarantee millions more illegals coming in, which is what hap-pened. To anti-immigration groups, it was the gift of a lifetime. They could point to it and say, "See? This is what those who are talking about immigration want. Amnesty."

They could not be further from the truth: what Dignity pro-poses is the opposite of amnesty. The Dignity Act is not amnesty, it's accountability. It says clearly: you broke the law, and you must make restitution. You must pay fines. You must contribute to training programs for Americans. You can never become an American citizen. You cannot receive federal benefits. You have to buy your own health insurance. The Dignity Act is not a free pass to those who snuck in. It stands for restitution, justice, and mercy in balance.

In my early days in Congress, based on the conversations I just described, I realized I was never going to get the far left or the far right on board. On one side, the far left wants blanket amnesty and will never accept restitution or limits on how people can come into the country. Nor was I going to win over the far right, the people who demand mass deportation of everyone by tomorrow morning, regardless of the economic or social consequences to the rest of the country.

It is also true that between those extremes lies a broad middle of members of both parties. In that middle is where solutions are forged for the benefit of the country. This is where most Americans are.

Every time I explained Dignity, I emphasized this: it is a calibrated compromise. It protects the border. It offers a legal path forward, but not citizenship, and not for free. It says: you can work, you will not be deported, you can go home for Christmas—but you must earn it. That is where the balance lies.

So what happens to the rare politician who proposes a compromise? You get hit from both sides. You have to fight a two-front war.

On the right, FAIR and NumbersUSA mobilize instantly. They unleash millions of dollars' worth of campaigns. They flood phone lines. They run ads against you in your own district. They brand you as soft, weak, a traitor to the cause. On the left, progressives do the same from the opposite side. If you do not back full citizenship and open borders, they accuse you of cruelty, racism, or betrayal.

That is exactly what happened to me. And I knew it would. But I did not come to Congress to keep my head down. I did not come here to be a politician. I came here to be a representative— of the American people. I came here to solve a problem. If that means taking the hits, so be it. I have won reelection twice by telling my constituents the truth.

I know what I am asking my colleagues to do. I am asking them to take a risk. I am asking them to have the courage to act.

As Speaker Mike Johnson, who the GOP is blessed to have, once told me privately: "The right thing to do isn't always easy, and the easy thing to do isn't always right." Immigration is precisely that kind of issue. It is complicated. It is divisive. But it is solvable—if we summon the courage.

Because the alternative is paralysis. The alternative is the cycle we've been stuck in for years: border open, border closed. Enforcement today, release tomorrow. A system that lurches from one president's executive order to the next.

We cannot live in fear forever.

The salience of this issue is once again at an all-time high. Public opinion is shifting. Many Americans are uneasy with mass deportations. They want enforcement, but they also want humanity. They want order, but they also want fairness. When long-standing neighbors are picked up and deported, people notice. When churches lose a third of their congregations, pastors notice. When employers cannot find workers, businesses notice. And when enough voices rise up, the political system eventually has to respond.

Even President Donald Trump has felt it. And he, too, recognizes that we need some of these long-term immigrants. He has cited the long-term construction and hospitality workers, specifically, but has gone beyond that, as well. In an interview with Rachel Campos-Duffy on *Fox Noticias* on April 15, 2025, he was asked about a man, Gelasio, who had lived in the United States for twenty years and had American-born children, he responded: "From a practical standpoint, yes, I look at this man, I say, 'This is a guy that we want to keep, right?' I mean, they'll probably take heat for saying it. Everybody wants everybody. That's a good man . . . I could see it just by looking."

So how do we get out of this mess?

The answer is the Dignity Act, the only serious immigration legislation sitting in Congress at this hour.

For the country, the result is strength, safety, and prosperity.

Dignity rests on the shoulders of the once-in-a-generation leadership of Donald J. Trump, the greatest political dealmaker of our time.

President Trump has the chance to do for immigration what Lincoln did for slavery and Reagan did for communism and the Cold War: bring a crisis to a historic conclusion.

The window is short. I'm also betting on the courage, wit, and humanity of my colleagues in Congress.

If we fail to act now, we may never get another chance.

The Promise of Dignity

- America can still solve big problems with boldness, vision, and fairness.
- Dignity secures the border, strengthens the economy, and restores trust in government.
- It is not only the right thing to do—it's the smart thing to do.
- This policy puts America, and Americans, first.
- Now is the time. Dignity is the way forward.

IMMIGRATION IS NOT A LIABILITY—IT'S AN OPPORTUNITY

On July 4, 2026, the United States will celebrate its 250th birthday. It's a big moment. And we have a big opportunity to set our course for the next 250 years. We can show the world what it means to be a nation that marries strength with mercy, law with grace, justice with faith.

That is the promise of Dignity. That is the promise of America.

The question is not whether Dignity reflects our values—it does. The question is not whether Dignity will be good for America—it will be.

I already have the support of business leaders, chambers of commerce, farmers, veterans, economists, immigration advocates, and faith leaders. But institutional support is not enough. Monumental, ambitious legislation requires more than endorsements; it requires people. It requires Americans to stand up, to speak out, to mobilize.

The real question is: when will everyday Americans rally for it?

Will it be only after their grocery bills climb higher and higher? After they see a coworker or a neighbor being arrested or deported? After their pastor tells them the church can no longer keep its doors open because half the congregation has been driven into the shadows?

When will the phones light up in Congress? When will town halls fill with angry constituents demanding answers? When will the pressure on Washington become unbearable?

When will Americans realize that immigration reform is not a liability—it is an opportunity? An opportunity to usher in a new golden age for America. What better moment than now, on the eve of our nation's 250th birthday?

WHY DO I—MARIA SALAZAR—CARE?

Many have asked what drives me in my fight for immigration reform. The answer is simple: to help make all Americans better off tomorrow than they were yesterday. To give Dignity to those living in the shadows. To expand the American Dream for all who believe in it.

I am an evangelical Christian, and empathy and compassion are at the heart of my faith. But this fight is not only about faith—it is also about preserving what has made America great.

I am a product of America's immigrant story. America took my family in when no one else would. My parents arrived in the United States as political refugees from Cuba with only five dollars in their pockets and the clothes on their backs. They were not given a single government handout. What they were given was opportunity—the chance to start over from the ground up, with the same opportunity available to everyone in the American system. Because of that, I am the product of the greatest country on earth. I made it to the United States Congress in only one generation.

The Cuban exiles were fortunate, maybe even an anomaly of history. We came at a time when Congress was engaged on immigration. We came at a time when refugees were seen as a strength during the Cold War. And we are the only immigrant group to have a special citizenship law: the Cuban Adjustment Act.

As a result of the 1966 Cuban Adjustment Act, Cuban Americans became the most privileged immigrant group in US history. The first wave of refugees—the solid middle-class Cubans who fled Fidel Castro's communist regime en masse in the 1960s and 1970s—built the city of Miami and transformed South Florida.

Today, Cubans control both the economy and the politics of that region. Cuban Americans now thrive in what I call a "ghetto of wealth." Wealthy Cuban girls marry wealthy American boys. (How disappointed my mother was that I didn't stick to the script! Always the rebel, I had to go off to become a war correspondent and then head to Congress...) They attend the University of Miami, become doctors, attorneys, and entrepreneurs, and build beautiful homes in a paradise called Miami. (By the way, I represent this amazing city in Congress.)

But many of us—the children of those exiles—carry a deeper legacy: the pain of loss, the trauma of leaving everything behind, the anxiety of not knowing the language, the instability of displacement, the fear of never finding work.

That is why, as a Cuban American, I feel called to use this position to help those less fortunate people seeking the same chance my family once received. Those seeking a dignified life in the Promised Land.

WHY DIGNITY IS GOOD FOR AMERICA

So yes, I am doing this because I believe it is the right thing to do—personally, morally, as a first-generation Cuban American and as a Christian. But I also believe it is the right thing to do for every American and for the future of this country.

To recap: the Dignity Act will grow GDP by trillions of dollars. It will increase tax revenues at every level of government. It will shore up Social Security and Medicare. It will help pay down our national debt.

By ending the shadow economy of under-the-table labor, we will raise wages for American workers and improve the quality of life for every citizen.

The Dignity Act will create hundreds of thousands of jobs, expand housing supply, and revitalize US manufacturing. It will strengthen our ability to compete with China, position us to lead in the global race for AI, and solidify American dominance in the twenty-first century.

Simply put, the Dignity Act means:

- More money in your pocket and billions in the US treasury
- Safer streets in your cities and communities
- Upholding our Judeo-Christian values

- The preservation of the American Dream (for your children and grandchildren) by growing the US economy for decades
- Bringing out of the shadows millions of people who could be our (good) neighbors
- Concentrating ICE resources to find the truly bad illegals

That is the promise of Dignity.

TIMING IS EVERYTHING

From the day I was elected to Congress, I have known what I wanted to do for the country. But in politics—as in life—timing is everything.

It is 2025, and we are standing at the edge of history.

For the first time in decades, the border is truly secure. In less than ninety days, President Trump fulfilled his promise, proving that it could, in fact, be done. Traffic to the southern border ground to a halt.

So to every Republican who has ever said, "Secure the border first, and then we'll talk about what to do with everyone already here"—that time has come.

For the first time, Democrats are feeling the consequences of the damage they did in the last four years at the border, and the decades of playing political football with the Hispanic community.

When the tragic murder of twenty-two-year-old nursing student Laken Riley—killed by an illegal immigrant who had previously been arrested but not deported—sparked national outrage, Congress acted. Lawmakers passed the Laken Riley Act, requiring ICE to detain illegal immigrants who had been *charged* with a crime—not convicted, just charged.

Nearly fifty Democrats in the House of Representatives voted for that bill—something unimaginable a decade ago. That vote is proof that we are living in a new reality. It is proof that Democrats, under mounting pressure to stop illegal immigration, can and will vote for measures that improve safety, like the Dignity Act.

Now is the time.

THREE NUMBERS

What we need comes down to three numbers: **218, 60, and 1.**

Two hundred and eighteen is the number of votes it takes to pass a bill in the House of Representatives. It doesn't matter if they're Republicans or Democrats. Two hundred and eighteen votes, and the bill moves forward to the Senate.

Sixty is the number of votes needed in the Senate. Today, there are fifty-three Republicans. That means at least seven Democrats must come on board. And they will, if we make the case clearly enough.

And that last number? **One.** One president. One man at the center of this moment: Donald J. Trump.

If President Trump says, *"I like this bill,"* everything changes. He can call Speaker Mike Johnson, Majority Leader Steve Scalise, and House Whip Tom Emmer—and tell them to bring the bill for a vote on the floor of the House of Representatives. (Someone close to them told me: "If you get the president to support this, I can get you the votes you need.")

I believe in Donald Trump because God appointed him to lead our nation, not once, but twice. He is the only one who can actually fix this because he has the guts to do it. He's a builder. He understands dealmaking. He is not afraid to push through what he believes is right, even if it's controversial.

We see—whether you agree with tariffs or not—a man who acts when he thinks America is being taken advantage of. That is leadership. That is courage. And immigration needs exactly that.

Here is the truth: The American people have been taken advantage of—by Washington politicians in both parties who let this crisis fester. The government has failed immigrants, yes, but it has also failed Americans—farmers, builders, dairies, slaughterhouses, factory workers, taxpayers—by creating a system full of injustice, hypocrisy, and broken incentives.

Here is another truth: this cannot be fixed by executive order. We cannot ping-pong policy back and forth every four years, depending on who sits in the White House. That chaos only makes things worse. One president signs protections; the next rips them away. One president expands enforcement; the next scales it back. The result is fear, confusion, instability, and families caught in the crossfire.

Right now, we are living in a contradiction. Politicians rail against illegal immigration, but at the same time, they look the other way because our economy relies on undocumented labor. Whether it's agriculture, construction, or hospitality, we depend on these workers—but we refuse to give them a path to legitimacy. We say, *"We're going to deport them,"* but then, when the backlash from worksite raids grows too intense, we quietly stop. Everybody knows it. And so the cycle repeats.

That's not leadership. That's dysfunction. It's time to stop pretending, stop kicking the can down the road, and fix this once and for all. We know they're here. We know who they are. We know what they contribute. We just refuse to deal with it.

What I am offering is a onetime good-faith fix. This isn't about punishing employers with jail time or staging mass round-ups. That's not realistic, and it's not practical. What is right is putting rules in place that say: *"You had your chance. We are making this legal—once, in good faith. But from this point on, the system works differently."*

No one else! No more jumping the fence at the border. No more working under the table. No more illegals coming into the United States.

Again, this is not for new arrivals. We are not rewarding people who just walked across yesterday. This is about the men and women who have been here for years—working, raising families, paying taxes, and building communities. We are going to bring them into the system legally. But we close the loopholes. We harden the border. We stop catch and release. After that, there are no excuses. Everyone knows the rules. Everyone gets one shot. And from then on, we enforce this new system with clarity and strength.

Republicans' biggest fear is simple: that if they agree to this, in ten years the country will be right back here again. This bill is different because we learned from our past mistakes. We are not offering temporary half-measures. We are not repeating the failures of our predecessors. This time, we are putting our money where our mouth is—making a once-in-a-generation investment in border security so it cannot be undone by executive whim, and building an immigration system that actually works.

This is not a Band-Aid. This is surgery. This is not a stopgap. This is permanence. This is dignity.

THE PROMISE OF DIGNITY

Now picture, one last time, a family.

Jose, a father, has been here for twenty years. He works hard. He built a small lawn care business—trucks, tools, steady clients. His wife, Rosa, puts in long hours at a restaurant. Together, they have three kids. Life has not been easy, but it is stable. Everything they have, they worked hard for.

And yet every night they go to bed with the same fear: *what if tomorrow it all disappears?*

Then one day, it does. ICE shows up. Jose is taken. Rosa is detained. The children—citizens by birth—are suddenly without parents. Where do they go? Not to family; there is no family close by. Not to foster care; the system is already overwhelmed. Maybe a neighbor takes them. Maybe a pastor. Maybe no one. Maybe they follow their parents to a country they have never even been to.

Their stability, their home, their childhood—all shattered in an instant today, right now. This is not fiction. This is not an exaggeration. This is what deportation looks like for countless families across America.

It isn't just Jose and Rosa. It is a story playing out again and again, in small towns and big cities, in farm fields and construction sites, in schools and churches. Once, enforcement was focused on criminals. Now, under mass deportation plans, it is ordinary people, who are just here working and keeping their heads down, caught in the net—neighbors, coworkers, classmates.

If, in the near future, the federal government insists on target-ing every undocumented person regardless of record, the ripple effects will be catastrophic. 8,800 American jobs lost for every 100,000 people deported. Slowing economic growth—per the Chair of the Federal Reserve himself. A recent Congressional Budget Office (CBO) correction showed sharp decreases in the labor force over the next ten years and increases in our deficit because of that.

It's not just numbers. Millions of lives upended. Thousands of families torn apart. Entire communities destabilized. And for what? To create fear, to play politics, to ignore the reality that our economy and our culture are already intertwined with these men and women.

That would not be law. That would be cruelty. And cruelty has no place in American greatness.

I have spoken with hundreds of undocumented immigrants. Let me tell you what I have learned. They are not sitting around thinking about politics. They are not scheming over loopholes or plotting to take advantage. They are in survival mode. They keep their heads down because they are hiding. One wrong move—a broken taillight, an expired tag—and their entire life could vanish.

It is one of the cruelest ironies we live with today. America shines as Ronald Reagan's "city on a hill," a beacon of freedom and hope to the world. We send our ideals abroad. We preach democracy and opportunity. But here at home, under our very noses, millions live in fear. Fear of a knock on the door. Fear of being torn from their families. Fear of a system that uses them and denies them dignity. It's true they snuck in, but someone gave them a job.

That is not just undignified. That is shameful. It is un-American. Shame on us.

Now you know the real truth. The nuances, the complexities, the depth of what our national conversation on immigration barely touches.

You also know that we are at a crossroads.

The choice we make here matters. Now is the moment of decision.

If we do nothing, here is what awaits us:

- Empty grocery shelves and higher food prices
- Hotels, restaurants, and farms without workers
- A stalled economy that cannot fill the jobs it needs
- A future president opening the border again
- Churches closing their doors
- Families left without caregivers
- America falling behind in manufacturing, technology, and innovation

- Rural communities hollowing out as businesses close
- Companies moving overseas
- Construction and housing shortages worsening
- Supply chains breaking down even further
- A declining quality of life and higher living expenses
- Invention and entrepreneurship slowing to a crawl
- Inflation and recession
- China rushing to seize the mantle of global leadership
- A weaker, divided America less able to lead the world

But if we act? If we summon the courage to pass the Dignity Act? Then here is what awaits us instead:

- Stronger communities
- Safer streets
- More jobs and higher wages
- Pay down our national debt
- No more future illegals coming in
- No more illegals getting federal benefits
- ICE can concentrate on the "bad *hombres*"
- DACA kids can become American
- Mixed-status families can stay together
- Improved quality of life for everyone
- An economy built to lead the twenty-first century
- Social Security and Medicare saved
- Secure borders with a system that actually works
- Farmers with the labor they need to keep food on America's tables
- Small businesses thriving instead of shutting down
- Innovation and entrepreneurship fueled by new talent
- A stronger America, able to lead the world with confidence

- A renewed promise of the American Dream, not just for immigrants, but for every citizen, for generations to come

Now is our chance to extend the promise that was once extended to me, to my family, to millions before us: the promise of Dignity.

Now is the time to do what every politician says they want but few have the courage to achieve: to truly make America great again.

Sources

American Action Forum. "Debunking Immigration Myths." May 13, 2021. https://www.americanactionforum.org/infographic /debunking-immigration-myths/.

American Immigration Council. "Fortune 500 Companies Founded by Immigrants, 2025." Accessed August 28, 2025. https://www.americanimmigrationcouncil.org/report/fortune -500-companies-founded-by-immigrants-2025/.

———. "New Data Shows Immigrant-Owned Businesses Employed 8 Million Americans, Immigrants Wield $1.1 Trillion in Spending Power." Accessed August 28, 2025. https://www .americanimmigrationcouncil.org/uncategorized/new-data -shows-immigrant-owned-businesses-employed-8-million -americans-immigrants-wield-1-1-trillion-in-spending-power/.

Associated Press. "Raid on Upstate New York Food Manufacturer Leads to Dozens of Detentions." 2025. https:// apnews.com/article/new-york-factory-raid-immigration -fbbe6dfb53eabc98e2f3277bdb7f81bc.

Beard Foundation, James. 2025 Independent Restaurant Industry Report: Resilience and Reinvention. New York: James Beard Foundation, 2025. https://www.jamesbeard. org/2025-independent-restaurant-industry-report.

Bier, David J. "Enforcement Didn't End Unlawful Immigration in the 1950s—More Visas Did." Cato Institute Blog, July 11, 2019. https://www.cato.org/blog/enforcement-didnt-end-unlawful-immigration-1950s-more-visas-did.

Bipartisan Policy Center. Green Light to Growth: Estimating the Economic Benefits of Clearing Green Card Backlogs. Accessed August 28, 2025. https://bipartisanpolicy.org/report/green-light-to-growth-estimating-the-economic-benefits-of-clearing-green-card-backlogs/.

Brnovich, Mark. "Biden Admin Has Decriminalized and Monetized Chaos at the Border: Kids Are Dying as a Result of Biden's Border 'Experiment,' Says the Arizona AG." Fox News, 2023. https://www.foxnews.com/media/mark-brnovich-biden-decriminalized-monetized-chaos-border.

Clemens, Michael A. "Trump's Proposed Mass Deportations Would Backfire on US Workers." Peterson Institute for International Economics (PIIE), March 6, 2024. https://www.piie.com/blogs/realtime-economics/2024/trumps-proposed-mass-deportations-would-backfire-us-workers.

Cruz, Melissa. "Why Is It So Hard to Become a US Citizen?" September 17, 2025. https://www.americanimmigrationcouncil.org/blog/is-it-hard-to-become-a-us-citizen.

Esterline, Cecilia. "How Immigrants Can Alleviate the Domestic Labor Shortage." Niskanen Center, November 21, 2022. https://www.niskanencenter.org/labor-shortages-shortfalls-in-the-domestic-labor-supply-and-why-immigrants-should-be-part-of-the-solution/.

Fox Charleston. "DHS Arrests Five Illegal Immigrants Convicted of Serious Crimes, Including Murder and Child Abuse." March 2024. https://www.foxcharleston.com/dhs-arrests-five-illegal-immigrants-convicted-of-serious-crimes-including-murder-and-child-abuse.

Fox News. "Migrant Caravan Containing Thousands Travels through Mexico toward US Border: 'Tell Biden We Are Coming.'" 2023. https://www.foxnews.com/politics/migrant-caravan-travels -mexico-towards-us-border-tell-biden.

———. "Migrant Caravan Demands Biden Administration 'Honors Its Commitments.'" 2023. https://www.foxnews.com /politics/migrant-caravan-biden-administration-commitments.

———. "Migrant in Potentially the Largest Caravan Ever Demands Biden Keep Asylum Promise." 2023. https://www.foxnews.com /world/migrant-largest-caravan-biden-promise-asylum.

———. "Migrant Caravan Heads toward U.S., Blinken Urges Mexico Help End Irregular Migration." 2023. https://www .foxnews.com/us/migrant-caravan-heads-toward-us-blinken -urges-mexico-help-end-irregular-migration.

———. "Nearly 8,000-Strong Migrant Caravan Heads Toward the US." 2023.

Fox News Video. "Growing Caravan Heads for US Border in Final Months of Biden Admin." 2023. https://www.foxnews .com/video/6365046606112.

Fox Wilmington. "Massive Identity Theft Scheme Led by Illegal Immigrants Uncovered after Raid at Meatpacking Plant." July 2023. https://foxwilmington.com/massive-identity-theft -scheme-led-by-illegal-immigrants-uncovered-after-raid-at -meatpacking-plant.

Guardian, The. "Federal Agents Blast Way into California Home of Woman and Small Children." June 27, 2025. https://www.theguardian.com/us-news/2025/jun/27 /california-home-raid-huntington-park.

———. "Iranian Woman, Who Has Lived in the U.S. for 47 Years, Taken by ICE While Gardening." June 27, 2025. https://www.theguardian.com/us-news/2025/jun/27/ice-detains -woman-iran-new-orleans.

———. "Small U.S. Towns Cancel Fairs Celebrating Latino Culture: 'The Climate of Fear Is Real.'" August 13, 2025. https://www.theguardian.com/us-news/2025/aug/13/small-towns-latino-fairs-ice-raids.

Holt, Eric A., and Bill Ray. The Skilled Labor Shortage and America's Housing Crisis: A Research Study by Home Builders Institute and University of Denver. Washington, DC: Home Builders Institute, May 2025. https://hbi.org/wp-content/uploads/2025/05/HBI-Denver-Study.pdf.

National Association of Evangelicals. One Part of the Body Report: The Potential Impact of Deportations on American Christian Families. March 31, 2025. https://www.nae.org/one-part-body-report-deportations-impact-christians-united-states/.

National Defense Industrial Association. "NDIA Letter on Immigration and Refugees." Press release, May 10, 2022. https://www.ndia.org/about/press/press-releases/2022/5/10/letter.

National Immigration Forum. "Undocumented Immigrants Are Integral to Our Nation." Accessed August 28, 2025. https://immigrationforum.org/article/undocumented-immigrants-are-integral-to-our-nation/.

Penn Wharton Budget Model. "Mass Deportation of Unauthorized Immigrants: Fiscal and Economic Effects." July 28, 2025. https://budgetmodel.wharton.upenn.edu/issues/2025/7/28/mass-deportation-of-unauthorized-immigrants-fiscal-and-economic-effects.

Rahman, Billal. "Florida Spent $660M on Health Care for Illegal Immigrants." Newsweek, March 13, 2025. Updated March 14, 2025. https://www.newsweek.com/florida-health-care-illegal-immigrants-2044101.

Reuters. "Chicago Protesters Defiant in Face of Trump's Deportation Threats." September 7, 2025. https://www

.reuters.com/world/us/chicago-protesters-defiant-face-trumps-deportation-threats-2025-09-07/.

———. "Dozens Detained in U.S. Immigration Raids in New York State, Governor Says." September 5, 2025. https://www.reuters.com/world/us/dozens-detained-us-immigration-raids-new-york-state-governor-says-2025-09-05/.

Shaw, Adam. "Tens of Thousands of Illegal Immigrants with Sexual Assault, Murder Convictions in US: ICE Data." Fox News, July 11, 2023. https://www.foxnews.com/politics/tens-thousands-illegal-immigrants-sexual-assault-homicide-convictions-roaming-us-streets.

Timm, Jane. "Meet the Grover Norquist of the Immigration Debate." MSNBC, December 4, 2012. https://www.msnbc.com/morning-joe/meet-the-grover-norquist-the-immigration-d-msna16510.

USAFacts. "What Can the Data Tell Us about Unauthorized Immigration?" Accessed August 28, 2025. https://usafacts.org/articles/what-can-the-data-tell-us-about-unauthorized-immigration/.

Watson, Tara. "How Immigration Reforms Could Bolster Social Security and Medicare Solvency and Address Direct Care Workforce Issues." Brookings Institution, April 16, 2024. https://www.brookings.edu/articles/how-immigration-reforms-could-bolster-social-security-and-medicare-solvency-and-address-direct-care-workforce-issues/.

Yahoo News. "ICE Arrests Almost 500 People at Hyundai Plant in Georgia." 2025. https://www.yahoo.com/news/articles/ice-arrests-almost-500-people-164438548.html.

———. "Small Town Rallies Around Soccer." Accessed August 28, 2025. https://www.yahoo.com/news/small-town-rallies-around-soccer-143123445.html.